concilium 1997/2

OUTSIDE THE MARKET NO SALVATION?

Edited by

Dietmar Mieth and
Marciano Vidal

SCM Press · London
Orbis Books · Maryknoll

Published by SCM Press Ltd, 9–17 St Albans Place, London N1
and by Orbis Books, Maryknoll, NY 10545

ISBN:0 334 03043 9 (UK)
ISBN:1 57075 127 7 (USA)

Typeset at The Spartan Press Ltd, Lymington, Hants
Printed by Biddles Ltd, Guildford and King's Lynn

Concilium Published February, April, June, October, December.

Contents

Editorial

The way the economy is organized – 'economic policy' – is going through a marked upheaval in this last decade of the twentieth century. On the one hand, the downfall of the economic systems based on Communist socialism ('real socialism') has been accompanied by a deep crisis in the welfare state within the liberal democracies: neither Communism – no longer effective – nor social democracy – internally weakened – can any longer provide the justificatory and guiding ideological underpinning for the economic policies of the present time. On the other hand, one of the most defining characteristics of the economy at the end of the twentieth century is undoubtedly its globalization. Interdependence has always been one of the constants of the economic world. But while in the past interdependence was limited in geographical extent and quantitative significance, today it embraces virtually the whole world and conditions all aspects of the economy.

Faced with this contemporary picture of the economic sphere, one would have hoped for the dawn of a new model of economic policy. But there is still no sign of any global alternative lightening the horizon. On the contrary, the capitalist model is tightening its grip through a return to pre-Keynesian *laissez-faire* liberalism – referred to, especially in Third World circles, as neo-liberalism (Couch). This hegemony of the capitalist economic model with a neo-liberal stamp has made us recall an old, disused theological axiom from ecclesiology: 'Outside the church there is no salvation.' Secularizing this axiom, we can ask, 'Is there no salvation outside capitalism?', understanding 'salvation' here as 'a more human economic alternative'.

Readers will observe that the title of this number of *Concilium* does not speak of 'capitalism' but of 'the market'. We have chosen to analyse the overall problem in terms of one of the elements or factors essential to present-day capitalism, the market. This, however, is not to take 'the market' in its neutral sense of the reality of economic life or as a category in the science of economics. We are considering it as set within an economic system, specifically within the capitalist economic system of the end of this century, marked as it is by the globalization of all aspects of human life.

The organization of the studies that make up this issue has been planned within an inter-disciplinary framework. The treatment is not strictly economic, nor strictly ethical, nor only theological. It sets out to provide a threefold consideration, thereby integrating the threefold argumentation that must characterize any ethical discourse on economics from theology: scientific argumentation, axiological argumentation and religious world-view (or argumentation). We must recognize that not every one of the studies presented here adopts this form of argumentation or reasoning. The nature of the aspect it analyses makes each incline more towards a particular line of argumentation. They need to be read as a whole to give a more accurate inter-disciplinary view.

The final contents of this number do reflect the initial plan overall. We have to recognize, nevertheless, that not every one of its four parts has been filled with all the subjects initially planned. It may be a help to readers if we outline the intention behind each of these parts.

1. *The market as an anthropological, social and economic reality.* Before passing any sort of value judgment on economic policy based on the market, we need to know how this mechanism of economic life and category of economic theory actually functions. Although it would have been interesting to analyse the workings of the market in the various evolutionary stages of the economy – pre-industrial, first industrialization, variations during the twentieth century – the articles in this first part concentrate on two types of approach: one overall, setting out its anthropological content and evaluating interpretations (Gómez Camacho); the other more specific, analysing the growth of the informal economy as an alternative form to the dominant capitalist system (Baum, Kern).

2. *The market and religion.* Religion has always been close to the economy: religious centres and centres of economic power have clearly been inter-related throughout history. At the same time, the economy has looked to religion to provide it with meaning, justification and guidance. The market and religion have also been closely connected. We had planned to analyse this inter-relationship by considering three major religious blocs: the market in Jewish prophecy; the market and Islam; the market in the great Eastern religions. This last study, by Bernard Teo, the only one which we were able to include, has not only a historical but also a present-day interest – showing the religious justifications still underlying economic activity today. Before it readers will find two articles on the relationship between the market and religion: one referring to the attitude in Christianity, taking both its Gospel sources and its present interpretations (Duchrow); the other referring to the situation of a single country, Cuba, still operating within the dictates of a collectivist economy (Houtart).

3. *The market and ethics.* Ethical consideration of economic systems

and the economy in general play a major part in present-day considerations of the world of economics. This presence of ethical discourse on the economy is as noticeable in moral philosophy as it is in theological ethics. Various axiological paradigms are used, most obviously ethical utilitarianism, functional pragmatism, the value of distributive justice, the option for the common good in individual terms and the proposal of radical justice in egalitarian terms. All these paradigms are examined and analysed in the three approaches selected to tackle the relationship between the market and ethics: the approach offered by papal social teaching (Hollenbach); the approach from those currents of thought that appear initially accepting of the market and capitalism (Lattuada); and the approach from liberation theology, which puts forward a radical critique of the present-day capitalist system (Dussel).

4. *The market and some challenges of the contemporary world.* The general considerations in the preceding parts are made specific in this section, applied to particular areas of human concerns. A particular option for a specific economic system has many implications. Opting for a market economy of a neo-liberal stamp conditions the workings of personal, interpersonal and social life. Reasons of space have obliged us to limit these specific considerations. We believe, however, that we have selected the major aspects of the overall reality: the structure of the state (Vidal); ecology (Fetscher); bio-technology (Mieth and Bompiani) and gender (Cahill).

The articles in this issue of *Concilium* do not claim to have reached any conclusive judgement on whether the market is good or bad, let alone on a particular form taken by it. Throughout its pages, readers will find judgments for it and – most – against it. The debate has to remain open. We hope it will be a debate carried on in the interests of the happiness of all, thinking first of all the weakest members of society.

Translated by Paul Burns

Dietmar Mieth
Marciano Vidal

I · The Market: An Anthropological, Social and Economic Reality

The Market: The History and Anthropology of a Socio-Economic Institution

Francisco Gómez Camacho

Introduction

Historical examination of the market reveals two schools: 1. those who, following Adam Smith, believe the market provides the 'natural' form of exchange among people, deriving from the equally 'natural' tendency human beings feel to exchange, to deal (which is what distinguishes human society from the animal kingdom); and 2. those who, with a more historical perspective, see in the capitalist free market only one historical, and so temporary, means of exchanging the goods and services which society needs for the subsistence of its members.

The first school looks for 'universal and eternal' laws that rule exchanges in the market, laws it sees as necessary to be able to qualify economic knowledge as scientific knowledge; it holds that this scientific basis is to be found in the known laws of supply and demand. It regards anything that deviates from these laws as mere voluntarism, as economic accidents without the least importance for scientific economics. The second school, on the other hand, gives these scientific accidents, which configure different stages in the scientific evolution of humankind, the scientific validity which the first claims to deny them. One of the schools that has most stressed this historical character of the capitalist market, besides the German historical school, is the Marxist school.

The market in history

The origins of the market, in the simplest and most basic meaning of the term as a place in which economic goods are traded, can be fixed at the very moment when trade was first carried on. In its modern sense a 'natural' institution capable of self-regulation, without the need for government intervention, it is only recently that it has acquired the social importance attributed to it today. Before the modern market existed, there was already division and specialization of labour, since even in the most primitive tribe there exists some division of function and the need to exchange the products of the work that has been carried out. But in this type of tribal society, it is custom that regulates both the division and assignation of labour and the distribution and exchange of products, even when this exchange involves covering great distances.

In the times of Classical Greece and the Roman Empire, what Polyani calls 'administered commerce' was practised. It was a 'splendid but insignificant' commerce,[1] and they were times in which economic practice had not yet become independent of social life but was rather at its service. One might say, in Aristotelian terms, that 'economy', understood in the sense of administration of the home, still dominated over 'crematistic', which sought only to increase wealth.

The practice of commerce was damaged by the fall of the Roman Empire and the subsequent rise of what we know as feudal society, a period in which the risks attendant on movement made the transportation of goods too dangerous. It was with the rise of cities and fairs in the twelfth century that merchants began a new period of economic development. Merchants then functioned as links between geographically distant communities and between very different cultures. A Spanish theologian, Tomás de Mercado, did not hesitate to praise the practice of this commerce in the sixteenth century as a unifying bond and source of information between peoples.[2] Local custom could no longer regulate the practice of international trade, and the practice of commerce was beginning to be seen as an independent and autonomous activity with respect to social life. As the same Tomás de Mercado wrote: 'Being a merchant is no longer being a man who seeks the good of his country as formerly, but being a great lover of money, and desirous of that of others.' This was the time when goods traded began to be seen as 'trade values' and not simply as 'use values'. It was also the period when the use of currency was extended and generalized, under the impulse of the arrival of precious metals (gold and silver) from Spanish America in the sixteenth century. The expansion of mercantile capitalism brought about a corresponding erosion of the bases of feudal society, and the first city-states became consolidated. These were the first nuclei of industrial and commercial capitalism. Its definitive triumph came with the industrial revolution and the work of a moral philosopher, Adam Smith, whose best-known work, *The Wealth of Nations* (1776), gave scientific support to the institution of the market. The freedom of the market gained ground throughout the nineteenth century, although not all nations accepted it to the same degree and extent. There were always those who saw the freedom of the market as an ideal difficult to achieve rather than as a reality to be preserved and respected, and there were nations which managed to harmonize, to a greater or lesser degree, the 'planned economy' alongside the 'free economy', thereby giving rise to the so-called 'mixed economies'.

The view of the market as a natural phenomenon, with an internal self-regulatory mechanism that allowed it to function as though it were a physical system independent of all human interference, has tended to obscure the earlier administrative tradition of political economy that developed in Classical Greece and remained in force throughout the Middle Ages and down to the work of Adam Smith. In the administrative tradition, human beings were seen as manipulators and regulators of economic activity, as administrators of their own economic affairs.[3] Smith's eclecticism allowed him to incorporate elements of both systems into his social and economic model: he followed the new tradition of the free market, self-regulated by the famous 'invisible hand', but he also followed the administrative tradition in dealing with fiscal problems and in seeing economics as a branch of moral philosophy and jurisprudence.

At the present time, when government spending in the developed countries of the West accounts for almost 50 per cent of GDP, it is hard to state that free-market economics predominates in these countries, though this does not prevent the free market from being one of the bases of economic activity formally recognized in their political constitutions. What seems undeniable is that the market today is one of the social and economic institutions that most divides the population into the two traditional groups: defenders and detractors of the free market, or – which comes to the same thing, but the other way round – defenders and detractors of state interventionism. These two positions are underpinned by two different views of human nature: positive and optimistic on the part of defenders of the free market, negative and pessimistic on the part of its detractors.

The market and human nature

At the present time, the market is one of those social institutions that seems to allow no neutral stance. Either you are in favour of the market, or you are against it; you can take it or leave it, but no intermediate position seems to be possible. The reason for the existence of this dilemma appears clear: the fate of the market is tied up with the fate of freedom and justice, and it is not possible to remain neutral on the subjects of freedom and justice: you are either in favour of them or against them. So when one speaks of the market, it is understood that one is speaking of a free market. This gives us the first anthropological root of this socio-economic institution we call the market: how in practice one understands freedom, especially in the conduct of economic affairs.

Its second anthropological root needs to be sought in epistemology, that is, in the theory of economic understanding. The market is generally seen by its defenders as a privileged place for access to the information we need in order to engage in economic activity, that is, to choose the economic conduct we consider best suited to the circumstances. Since it is not possible to want and choose what we do not know, the information we need to be able to choose on the basis of knowledge is provided for us by the market and – more precisely – by the prices freely determined in the market. Liberal economic thinking supposed an optimistic epistemology in Karl Popper's sense. It supposed that economic truth is plain to all those who have recourse to the market, and that no (religious or political) intermediaries are needed to know this truth: economic truth is plain to all equally in the prices determined by the forces of supply and demand in the free market. Just as citizens who vote in a democracy are never mistaken in rejecting and electing those who govern them, neither are those who 'vote' in the market mistaken in choosing what they want to buy or sell. It would be as absurd to deny the rightness of markets as it would be to deny the rightness of ballot-boxes in a democratic system. The rightness of the market was and is therefore the supreme norm for economists who uphold free trade.

The nineteenth century witnessed social struggles to implant respect for this supreme norm of liberal economic thought, and also the opposition it met with among the working classes. The workers were not at all optimistic with regard to the truth supplied by the market, and even less so with regard to its democratic character. In the twentieth century, the socio-economic and political conflicts of the period between the two World Wars brought about, among other things, a decrease in optimism with regard to the truth of the market. At the same time, a pessimistic epistemology was emerging, and after the First World War this took shape in Keynesian economic theory. The economic ideas put forward by Keynes were based on an anthropology distinct from that of classical liberalism. Freedom of the individual had to be a wisely controlled freedom, since the knowledge possessed by individuals was not always socially correct. Keynes saw human nature with eyes different from those of the school of Adam Smith, and so wrote in the *General Theory*:

> The task of transmuting human nature must not be confused with the task of managing it. Though in the ideal commonwealth men may have been taught, or inspired or bred to take no interest in the stakes [investing on the Stock exchange], it may still be wise and prudent statesmanship to allow the game to be played, subject to rules and limitations, so long as the average man, or even a significant section of the community, is in fact strongly addicted to the money-making passion.[4]

The Keynesian economics that dominated after the Second World War was a paternalistic economics to the extent that it considered economic knowledge as an elite knowledge, needed by some supposedly privileged mediators in order to interpret the interests of society correctly. Against the epistemological optimism of liberalism, which trusted in the 'objective' messages that came from the free market, the Keynesians shared a pessimistic epistemology with respect to the market, that is, with respect to those individuals who have recourse to it in order to choose, by voting with their money, the product or services that gives them the best social return. In Keynesian theory, economic and social truth are not clear to all citizens in the same way and with the same objectivity. There exist social and economic circumstances that give rise to privileged information and, by the same token, to erroneous information. The truth that leads to the common good of society no longer proceeds from the market and those who have recourse to it; it requires the mediation of a privileged understanding, which can naturally be none other than the understanding of the state, of government authority or, more often, that of its economic advisers.

A logical consequence of accepting this superior wisdom attributed to the state and its economic advisers is to furnish them with the means necessary to apply this wisdom. The two most efficacious instruments Keynes gave them were, in a way, those that Adam Smith had denied to mercantilist governments at the end of the eighteenth century: monetary policy and fiscal policy. Governments would once again be able to decide the amount and the value of money in circulation; they could also use taxes to achieve the goals they had, for the good of society, paternalistically defined for economic policy.

So since the end of the Second World War, and as far as confidence in the market is concerned, we have returned to a situation analogous to that of the mercantilism of the seventeenth and eighteenth centuries. The mercantilist policies which Adam Smith and classical economists had criticized for being based on arbitrary state intervention in the 'natural' processes of the economy are once more seen in a favourable light. Confidence in the regulatory power of Smith's 'unseen hand' was replaced by confidence in the wisdom and power of governments, now more concerned to reconcile the opposed interests of capital and labour in the short term than was the invisible hand, which was concerned only with long-term reconciliation. Once more, the problem of making the common interests of society compatible with the interests of individuals was posed, and the regulatory function that *laissez-faire* liberals had cheerfully left to the free market was now – no less cheerfully – assigned to the activity of the state. The architect of this change of mentality, as I have indicated, was none other than John Maynard Keynes, who in his *General Theory* provided governments with the theoretical bases for the intervention in the economy that Adam Smith had denied them.

The Keynesian economics that has inspired the economic policies of the West in the second half of the twentieth century protected the vulnerable members of society, especially by offering social security to those involuntarily out of work, and security of employment to those in work, in a way that the free market could not guarantee. This can explain the growing acceptance of a view of economic management that offered higher levels of security and welfare at the cost of renouncing increased levels of freedom. To the extent that the loss of economic freedom went hand in hand with economic growth and full employment society kept its faith in the wisdom and ability of governments to guarantee stable levels of economic and social welfare.

In the last decades, however, the situation has changed, and not only because the fall of the Berlin Wall has led to the exposure of the historic errors of Communist governments with planned economies. The conditions that made sustained growth and full employment possible in the Western countries have also disappeared, while inflationary processes have accelerated, or, in the best cases, continued. This change was bound to affect the confidence placed in the economic wisdom and policy of the State; and – more significantly for a correct understanding of the crisis the Welfare State is currently going through – the economic actions of governments are actually seen as sources of uncertainty and, therefore, generators of economic insecurity. This uncertainty and insecurity generated in the economy by governments is, amongst others, one of the reasons that explain the present crisis of the Welfare State. Once again in the history of the human race, there is a conflict between planning and freedom – in this case, between government planning and individual freedom.

As we approach the close of the twentieth century, however, this conflict between planning and freedom has developed a new aspect that makes it a qualitatively different conflict: we have now discovered the limitations of both contenders. Neither does government planning merit the confidence we formerly placed in it, nor has individual freedom recovered the esteem it enjoyed in the past and which it effectively lost in the twentieth century.

If this century began with a wounded individual freedom in need of healing, its last decades are witnessing how the wound now affects state planning. Society, which entered our twentieth century seeing damage being done by mistrust to one of its basic pillars, freedom, is, at the end of this same century, seeing another of its basic pillars, state planning, apparently damaged by the same mistrust. The compromise between individual freedom and social concern that underpinned the social contract in previous ages needs to be renewed, but on new premises capable of suppressing the suspicions that have developed between the two pillars over the past two centuries. On the medium- and long-term horizon, however, there is still no sign of what these new premises might be. I certainly do not believe that the new alliance we need between economic freedom and planning can in any way be achieved simply by amplifying the geographical spread of the market. To replace national boundaries with geographically wider zones of trade integration, even on a world-wide scale, will do no more than postpone the exacerbation of the crisis; it cannot avoid it. A strategy based on broadening markets might be able to broaden the scope for individuals to experience a provisional freedom and, in the same way, for a hypothetical governmental authority to apply its planning, but it will do nothing to resolve the problem of mutual mistrust that exists today between economic freedom and planning. We seem to be facing not a problem of quantity or geographical extension of economic life or activity, even if levels of unemployment suggest this, but a problem of quality or qualitative change in this economic life and activity. It is possible that we may be facing a social and economic situation in which the wisest course might be to posit the desirability, perhaps the necessity, of establishing the social bases for bringing about the society and economic system that classical economists called 'steady state', and which, in the dynamic of history, some of them (John Stuart Mill, for example) viewed as a social situation preferable to that of sustained economic growth. Keynes referred to such a situation when he visited Spain in 1930.

During this visit he gave a lecture which he titled 'The Economic Possibilities for our Grandchildren'. This was one of the few occasions when Keynes set his sights on the long term, and with this long-term view he described a world in which the economic problem of scarcity would have been overcome, with the result that we would be able to listen happily to 'the voice of morality'. When this world arrived, Keynes wrote in 1930:

> When the accumulation of wealth is no longer of high social importance there will be great changes in the code of morals. We shall be able to rid ourselves of many of the pseudo-moral principles which have hag-ridden us for two hundred years, by which we have exalted some of the most distasteful of human qualities to the position of the highest virtues. We shall be able to afford to dare to assess the money-motive at its true value. The love of money as a possession – as distinguished from the love of money as means to the enjoyments and realities of life – will be recognized for what it is, a somewhat disgusting morbidity, one of those semi-criminal, semi-pathological propensities which one hands over with a shudder to the specialists in mental disease. All kinds of social customs and economic practices affecting the distribution of wealth and of economic rewards and penalties, which we now maintain at all costs, however distasteful and unjust they may be in themselves, because they are tremendously useful in promoting the accumulation of capital, we shall be free, at last, to discard.[5]

Economists have always seen the phase of capitalist expansion as a transitional phase, of longer or shorter duration, towards what is known as a steady state, and the society Keynes envisages for his grandchildren corresponds to this same idea of a society in which selfish motives for accumulating capital are no longer necessary and can be abandoned in favour of a 'moral' economic policy. In the future to which Keynes looks, as in the classic steady state, we shall have reached the end of the rule of need, and economic conduct can be the expression of a world ruled by freedom and morality; it will therefore have a gratuitous character. This will then be when we can act from solidarity and take care of other people. In this new future society, Keynes says, 'I see us free, therefore, to return to some of the most sure and certain principles of religion and traditional virtue – that avarice is a vice, that the exaction of usury is a misdemeanour, and the love of money is detestable, that those walk most truly in the paths of virtue and sane wisdom who take least thought for the morrow.'

Finally, once we are in the new society, we shall be able to 'value ends above means and prefer what is good to what is useful'. But for the present, Keynes warned in 1930, we should not be too starry-eyed, because, 'The time for all that is not yet. For at least the next hundred years we must pretend to ourselves and to every one that fair is foul and foul is fair; for foul is useful and fair is not. Avarice and usury and precaution must be our gods for a little longer still. For only they can lead us out of the tunnel of economic necessity into daylight.'[6]

The promised land is within sight, but we have not reached it yet. For Keynes, unlike Marx, its coming will 'be produced gradually, not as a catastrophe', but we shall end up by reaching this new land. And, in an expression that seems to have been drawn from apocalyptic theology, Keynes exclaims: 'In truth [the new society] has begun.'

Conclusion

The society Keynes forecast for his grandchildren was a society in which economic abundance provided the necesssary condition for the practice of virtue and solidarity; a bourgeois society in which only after filling their stomachs could people think, in freedom, of sharing what is left over with others. It was a society in which the rule of need would have been conquered by the selfish forces of capitalist accumulation and could then prescind from the capitalist market as the channelling institution for assigning resources and distributing goods. In such a society, economic conduct would not have to be based on maximizing usefulness for oneself and could be replaced by conduct based on morality. Truly human ends could be put before material ends and morality would take precedence over individual selfishness. Such a society would, no doubt, be preferable to present-day society, in which economic conduct is governed by the rule of need.

What we need to ask ourselves is how far we are able – and willing – to bring forward this ideal of society glimpsed by economists; to what extent the practice of solidarity is necessarily tied to the elimination of want. Looking to the future, this seems to be the challenge humanity has to face: to tackle the essential task of harmonizing behaviour based on solidarity with overcoming economic need – which cannot be delayed. On the reply society is prepared to give to this question will depend how much can be hoped for from the market as a social and economic institution. As things are, it seems we cannot much longer ignore the need to introduce greater solidarity into the economic relationships with which we aspire to resolve the problem of economic need.

Translated by Paul Burns

Notes

1. K. Polanyi, *The Great Transformation: The Political and Economic Origins of Our Time*, Boston 1957.
2. T. De Mercado, *Suma de Tratos y Contratos*, Seville 1571, Book 2, ch. 2; modern ed. in 'Clásicos de Pensamiento Económico Español', Madrid 1977.

3. S. Todd Lowry, *The Archaeology of Economic Ideas: The Classical Greek Tradition*, Durham 1987.

4. J. M. Keynes, 'The General Theory of Employment, Interest and Money', Vol. VII, Ch. 24, 1, of the *Collected Writings of J. M. Keynes*, London and Cambridge 1973.

5. J. M. Keynes, *Essays in Persuasion*, London 1936, 369.

6. Ibid., 371–2.

A Colossus with Clay Feet.
Is the World Economy about to Collapse?

Bruno Kern

In my view there is no point in engaging in ideological trench warfare over 'the market'. Hardly anyone will dispute today that market mechanisms have an indispensable function in so far as they are embedded in a more comprehensive institutional framework, a field which does not have the form of a market. However, what has formed in world history and finally established itself all over the world is a capitalist market economy, the logic of which determines all other spheres of life. The immanent mechanisms of this kind of market economy and the way in which it conflicts with basic interests of life and survival are discussed at least in part elsewhere in this issue, so they need be referred to only briefly here. My main concern will be to examine the dynamic which in my view stamps the global economic system most clearly today and which plays an essential part in its self-destructive tendencies: the process of detaching the monetary levels from the real economy, i.e. from the actual exchange of goods and services.

I. The ideological character of the capitalist economy

The economy is ideological not only in the sense of the prevailing theory, but also in the sense of the real economic process. It is ideological in that it systematically leaves fundamental reality out of account. The mechanism of growth[1] immanent in it abstracts from the physical conditions of our existence, from the finitude of our natural resources, from real needs. The natural conditions of existence, the consumption of energy and material, are external to the logic of the capitalistic market, as are real needs in so far as they do not correspond to a quantifiable demand (purchasing power) to which alone it is capable of reacting. Natural resources, which are not produced by the capitalistic market, are treated as though they were unlimited. But the social field, the political institutions and the cultural world are also systematically 'consumed'. With its built-in disproportion between the power of the immediate producers and that of the owners of the means of production, which has a tendency to increase on the ideological pretext that in principle all participants in the market are equal and thus in the long term concentrates capital, the logic of the market undermines any claim to democracy.

The predominant neo-liberal theory ultimately reflects only this process of abstraction from the real economy. The supposed tendency towards equilibrium can be refuted both empirically and systematically. The latter has been done above all by F. J. Hinkelammert.[2] As for the empirical side, one must ask with E. Altvater, 'Where on the globe are there market economies which keep the classical promise of rationality, prosperity and freedom?'[3]

II. Casino capitalism

However, the prevailing contradiction in the global economic system today is the decoupling of the monetary level from the real economy. Only a bare 2% of the turnover on the international stock markets (which daily amounts to ten times the currency·reserves of the ten leading economic countries) serves to finance imports and exports, an exchange of goods and services which actually takes place. The 'remaining' 98% is a speculative overhang. Thus decisive data for the real economy, like currency rates, are governed by speculation.[4]

This historical development has ultimately been made possible by the twofold function of money as both a means of circulation and a means of payment. Whereas in its function as a means of circulation it is tied to the real economy, as a means of payment it develops a life of its own independent of this; in its turn it becomes a commodity, the price of which is interest. The hierarchy of interest and profit has nowadays been reversed: in other words, interest has become the decisive parameter for the world economy and governs the space available for the distribution of income and profitability. In a situation in which interest yield became more certain than profit, there has developed what economists call casino capitalism. Thus for example in the USA the interest rate is more than twice the growth rate. Even in the Federal Republic of Germany, the growth rate in incomes as wealth clearly exceeds all other growth rates (income from paid work or capital employed in production). This also expresses a redistribution in favour of those in possession of wealth.[5]

The capitalization of interest, i.e. compound interest, is a decisive contradiction to the presuppositions of the real economy. The irrationality of this mechanism becomes clear through extrapolation into the future. A model calculation cited by Karl Marx himself in the third volume of *Das Kapital* can illustrate this: 'Money that bears compound interest initially grows slowly, but as the rate of growth continually accelerates, after some time it becomes so rapid that it mocks any imagination. A penny lent at the birth of our Redeemer at compound interest of 5% would now have grown to a sum larger than would be contained in 150 million earths, all made of pure gold.'[6]

The mechanism of compound interest represents an exponential curve. It would ultimately be compatible with the real economy only if it were matched by an exponential growth in the real economy. Theoretically, the rate of compound interest may not exceed the economic growth-rate if the cycle of borrowing, making a profit and discharging debts, is to function. Therefore the inevitable consequence of the automatism of compound interest is either inflationary processes or an inability to pay and a corresponding automatism of debts in large parts of the economy. For reasons of space I can refer here only to the relevant analyses by economists like F. J. Hinkelammert or H. Creutz, who show that automatic compound interest is the real driving force behind compulsive growth, the pressure towards a permanent over-use of resources, inflationary processes and a constantly increasing gap between those with wealth and those forced into poverty. A historical examination makes it clear that the automatism of debts caused by compound interest has never been resolved in a purely economic way, but always in a way that has been political in some form (which among other things can mean war). Evidently there is a paradox here: only because the monetary balloon regularly bursts can we use the system of compound interest at all.[7]

Against the background of the international debt crisis which became manifest for the first time in 1982, when Mexico declared its inability to pay, in what follows the irrationality and danger of the automatism of debt should become evident.

III. Monopoly with corpses

Clearly the whole complex web of causes of the debt crisis (e.g. the internal causes in the countries concerned) cannot be analysed here. We shall limit ourselves to the aspect relating to the contradictions of the international finance system.

In my view it is already misleading to speak of the debt crisis of the 'Third World' (in addition today, of course, we have the historically socialist countries). This is essentially a crisis for the international system of finance as a whole, and its consequences are primarily being foisted one-sidedly on the Third World countries.

The first crisis of post-war capitalism in the industrial countries stands at the beginning of the debt crisis. Wages orientated on productivity and the resultant mass purchasing power made possible the post-war 'economic miracle'. In the middle of the 1960s the immanent limits of this dynamic became visible for the first time. Because of the cost of wages orientated on productivity, the rates of profit fell in the industrial countries, the markets began to get satiated and as a consequence the rate of investment declined. A 'crisis of excessive liquidity' became evident, i.e. a release of financial capital which could no longer be used productively. The banks had the task of using this surplus capital profitably. The Eurodollar market which arose in the 1950s, i.e. dollar credit business by European private banks beyond the control of the central banks (which reduced the cost of credit etc. by the abandonment of an obligatory minimum reserve), played a major role here. In 1983 more than 700 billion US dollars which were invested in the Eurodollar market came from transnational concerns (the so-called metrodollar). This tendency was merely intensified at the beginning of the 1970s by the petrodollars, the surplus money from the OPEC countries at the beginning of the first oil crisis. The credit-hungry developing countries presented themselves as a profitable use for the money. The drug of cheap credit – to use Altvater's term – was thrown on to the market until the dependence was total.[8]

The 'surplus' of financial capital which accumulated in the 1970s, the proceeds of exports and interest yields which could no longer be reinvested, at the same time set off a wave of speculation which developed into one of the most dangerous processes in the Western market system. Parallel to the process of falling into debt there developed a historically unprecedented speculation in property and shares which had its centre above all in Japan (alongside the USA and Great Britain).[9]

However, the international debt crisis must not least be described as the crisis of the leading capitalist power, the USA. It was first able to safeguard its leading economic role through the Bretton Woods Agreement (1944). In the course of the first post-war decades, however, the USA increasingly forfeited this role (in favour of Japan and Germany). A constant deficit in the US balance of payments gave rise to anxiety about world trade based on the dollar and possible marketing on this basis. The Vietnam war, which to a large extent was financed by printing money, was a reinforcing factor. To preserve the capacity for competition there was finally no alternative but to abandon the Bretton Woods Agreement (the dollar on the gold standard and a system of fixed rates of exchange) one-sidedly and *de facto* devalue the dollar.

From the beginning of the 1980s an enormous domestic deficit was added to the deficit in the balance of trade and payments – above all because of immense spending on armaments and a government policy which favoured high-tech and transnational capital. To cover its deficits, in the 1980s the US administration resorted to the instrument of a high-interest policy. High rates of interest were meant to guarantee attractive conditions for foreign investors. On the international credit markets this meant direct competition with the developing countries which were in debt. In 1981 the leading interest rate zoomed to a level above 21%. For the developing countries, who largely had taken credit with variable rates of interest which changed with the market situation, this was fatal. The debt trap snapped shut. A high interest rate resulted directly in a high exchange-rate for the dollar (because of the demand for the dollar by foreign investors) and this hit the developing countries, whose debts were usually in dollars, doubly hard. At the same time it posed an insoluble dilemma to the USA: a high rate of exchange for the dollar in turn undermined its competitive position and increased the balance-of-trade deficit. As early as the middle of the 1980s the economist A. Schubert described this dilemma in a way which found its sorry confirmation with the second Gulf War.[10]

The change of course in US monetary policy since the end of the 1980s is in no way to be seen as a correction but rather as a consistent second phase of the same policy, which was now concerned to safeguard what had been achieved, i.e. above all to make it possible for the debtor countries to have export surpluses in order to ensure their capacity to pay.[11] New credits served above all to service old debts – a fatal economic vicious circle. In many countries the quota for servicing debts, i.e. the proportion of export proceeds used in servicing debts, amounted to 40% and more. Even those with little knowledge of economics can easily imagine what this meant for the economies of such countries. As a result of the servicing of debt the paradoxical situation arose that from 1984 on the developing countries were net capital exporters to the industrial countries. Every year on average around 50 billion dollars more was transferred from the developing countries to the industrial countries than vice versa. Above all, the systematically propagated strategy of debt-to-equity swaps to relieve debt made it clear what the crisis management of the creditor countries and their multilateral organizations were concerned with: under the pressure of foreign debt important parts of economies were sold off, and nationalized key industries and infrastructures (telecommunication, transport net-works, etc.) were privatized. The debt crisis, and as a result of it the intensive pressure towards currency management, are today the main cause of the ecological destruction, the exclusion of large parts of the population from economic and social life, the de-industrialization and reduction of many threshold countries to raw material exporters and the cementing of dependent conditions. But the economies of the North are also among the losers in this process. It has been almost exclusively the creditor banks which have profited.[12]

IV. The Pyrrhic victory of capitalism

Robert Kurz, above all, has brought out in compelling analyses the tendency of the world economic system towards collapse.[13] Basically, he understands failed historical socialism and the developed capitalism of the Western industrial countries as two genres of the consumer society which he follows Karl Marx in describing as essentially 'fetishistic'. He interprets the downfall of real socialism in terms of the contradictions of this consumer society as a whole and therefore understands it as an anticipation of the collapse of the capitalist world economy generally. The globalization of the economy accelerates the process of competition between the different levels of productivity. Here an attempt by economies with lower productivity to catch up is like the race between the hare and the tortoise. The economies of the Third World and the former 'real socialist' societies have no chance of attaining the level of productivity of the world market. Each new round of the competitive process means an annihilation of capital on a large scale, and with it also an annihilation of capacity to pay and purchasing power. In this way capital undermines its own basis for use. In destroying the productivity which is no longer capable of being competitive, it also destroys the purchasing power which could have derived from this, and the markets for its own products in increasingly large areas of the world. The internal contradictions of the process of the accumulation of capital can no longer be overcome by opening up new markets. According to Kurz, the debt crisis is simply a provisional substitution of the purchasing power that has been destroyed. From this perspective he analyses two deficit cycles, one in Europe and the other in the Pacific, each with its surplus countries, Germany and Japan (along with the Asian 'four little tigers'). For years they have been financing their own export surpluses by giving credit themselves. The two deficit cycles are ultimately connected. The Western countries in deficit – headed by the USA, whose foreign debt at the end of the Reagan era was estimated at $500 billion – not only pay for their imports with credits from the surplus countries, Germany and Japan, but also indirectly finance the debt-servicing of the loser economies of the South and East through the international finance markets.

More and more states and regions are hopelessly going under in the accelerated global competition with its imperative of higher productivity. More and more purchasing power is being destroyed, and this can only laboriously be artificially replaced by credits. The 'superstructure of speculation' since the over-liquidity at the beginning of the 1970s, which has developed out of the 'credit superstructure', plays a role here which is not to be underestimated. The global mountains of debt would not be financed from the export surpluses alone. This part of the speculation in particular gives cause to fear an accelerated chain reaction, a domino effect. In the end the basic process of the global annihilation of purchasing power through productivity which is 'too high' cannot be stopped. 'If the last slim thread between real accumulation and credit superstructure snaps, the whole of speculation must come crashing down.'[14] Kurz points out indications that the limits of the substitution of credit finance for purchasing power are being reached. Moreover the third and last debt crisis, that of the Western deficit economies themselves, would pull the supposed victors, Germany and Japan, down into the abyss and spark off a world economic crisis of an unprecedented extent.

In the face of these gloomy perspectives of course the question arises whether the market can be regulated and political counter-pressure applied.[15] This is a question which cannot be developed here; a reference to relevant works must suffice. The title of this article might be a first indication of how this fundamental crisis of the capitalistic world economic system and the possibility of a catastrophic collapse in it might be tackled in theological and spiritual terms.

Translated by John Bowden

Notes

1. It should be noted here that even the 'social market economy' does not tame this compulsion towards growth; on the contrary, its functioning presupposes a long-term quantitative growth. So the social-ecological market economy which is also propagated a great deal today is a contradiction in terms. Cf A. Müller-Armack, 'Soziale Martkwirtschaft', in *Handwörterbuch der Sozialwissenschaften* 9, Göttingen 1965, 390–2.

2. F. J. Hinkelammert, *Kritik der utopischen Vernunft. Eine Auseinandersetzung mit den Hauptströmungen der modernen Gesellschaftstheorien*, Lucerne and Mainz 1964, 62–106.

3. E. Altvater, *Die Zukunft des Marktes. Ein Essay über die Regulation von Geld und Natur nach dem Scheitern des 'real existierenden Sozialismus'*, Münster 1991, 97.

4. J. Huffschmid, 'Tobin-Steuer: Die ernsthafte Diskussion beginnt', in *WEED-Informationsbrief Weltwirtschaft und Entwicklung*, September 1996, 1; *epd-Dritte-Welt Information* 11/11 (July 1996) is very informative on the various forms of speculation (derivatives like futures, options, deals on the forward market, etc.).

5. Altvater, *Zukunft des Marktes* (n. 3), 148ff.; U. Duchrow, *Alternativen zur kapitalistischen Weltwirtschaft. Biblische Erinnerung und politische Ansätze zur Überwindung einer lebensbedrohende Ökonomie*, Gütersloh and Mainz 1994, 82.

6. *Marx/Engels Werke* 25, 408.

7. F. J. Hinkelammert, 'Der Schuldenautomatismus', in '. . .*in euren Häusern liegt das geraubte Gut der Armen'. Ökonomisch-theologische Beiträge zur Verschuldungskrise*, with contributions by Kuno Füssel, Franz Hinkelammert, Markus Mugglin, Raul Vidales, Fribourg and Brig 1989, 79–190; H. Creutz, *Des Geldsyndrom. Wege zu einer krisenfreien Marktwirtschaft*, Berlin 1993.

8. Cf. above all A. Schubert, *Die internationale Verschuldung. Die Dritte Welt und das transnationale Bankensystem*, Frankfurt am Main 1985, 9–81.

9. R. Kurz, *Der Kollaps der Modernisierung. Vom Zusammenbruch des Kasernensozialismus zur Krise der Weltökonomie*, Leipzig 1994, 274f. According to estimates by the German Federal Bank the amount from the profits of productive and finance capital which is not reinvested but wanders around the world finance markets looking for speculative possibilities of investment amounts to 150 billion DM per year.

10. 'The development of the world monetary market in the last ten years shows clearly that the USA is not ready to give up exploiting the economic resources of the states integrated into its "security system" in favour of an equitable economic development of these nations. On the one hand this sharpens the tendency of the world economy towards crisis. On the other hand it expresses an almost reckless concern to maintain power which includes the readiness for military intervention in all parts of the world . . . Enormous amounts are spent on armaments in the USA, and the budget deficits which result from this are financed with foreign capital. Meanwhile the industrial competitive situation in many other areas is jeopardized. If this development continues, its necessary consequence will be that one day the USA will be forced to put this armament production to a "useful" purpose . . . ' (Schubert, *Internationale Verschuldung* [n. 8], 113–14). Among other things the monetary policy of the USA also needs to be analysed from an internal economic perspective, bringing out the deliberate concentration of capital which results in its redistribution in favour of armaments, high-tech and transnational capital. Thus e.g. H. Schui, *Die Schuldenfalle. Schuldenkrise und Dritte-Welt-Politik der USA*, Cologne 1988.

11. H. Schui, 'Verschuldung der Dritten Welt und internationale Kapitalstrategien', in Institut für marxistische Studien und Forschungen. Antiimperialistisches Solidaritätskomitee (ed.), *Die Dritte Welt in Schuldenkrise*, Frankfurt am Main 1986, 23–25.

12. See above all B. Kern, 'Warum ernährt das Kalb die Kuh? Die internationale Verschuldungskrise: eine bankrotte Weltwirtschaft auf Kosten der Armen', in Missionszentrale der Fransziskaner (ed.), *Internationale Verschuldungskrise*, Berichte – Dokument – Kommentare 35, Bonn 1989, 22f. The strategy of debt-to-equity swaps is propagated among other things in the Santa Fe Secret Document II putting forward guidelines for George Bush's foreign policy: 'Geheimdokument von Santa Fe II, Der Imperialismus vor Lateinamerika', *envio* 90, 1988, 25. S. George, *Der Schuldenbumerang. Wie die Schulden der Dritten Welt uns alle bedrohen*, Reinbek 1993, has given an impressive analysis of the way in which the debt crisis rebounds on the economies of the creditor countries.

13. Cf. above all Kurz, *Kollaps der Modernisierung* (n. 9).

14. Ibid., 277.

15. See here above all Duchrow, *Alternativen zur kapitalistischen Weltwirtschaft* (n. 5), 202–301, and the literature cited there.

Liberation: A Biblical Vision
I Samuel 1.1 – 2.11

Beatriz Melano Couch

Introduction

We will divide this Bible study into two parts, each of equal importance:
I. The historical context of Hannah's family and of Israel in her time;
II. Its contextualization for the people of God today. The historical
literary context will help us understand better what this story with its
song means to women today and to peoples around the world in the
conglomerate package of complaint, yearning, despair and search for
hope, assurance, empowerment amidst the gross and rampant dehumanization as our millennium comes to an end.

This marvellous text gives us a vision of God's sovereign events in
creation and in history, and it invites us to have the courage to claim a
power that is longed for and summoned into being by lowly human
beings with no special capacity or virtue but simply a stubborn insistence on believing and hoping that God's almighty power may prevail
in their individual lives and in the destiny of the people.

Where faith and praise acknowledge God's sovereignty over all, his
mighty power to change what seems irreversible in any area (historical,
political, social, sexual, racial, ecological), this act is accompanied by
true faith beyond limits, hope and commitment. The future changes:
new life, new beginnings are opened for individuals around the world.
This newness becomes possible in spite of the surrounding events which
seem to shatter all possibilities, where God's recreative and redemptive
action seems unimaginable (as in Rwanda, the 'dirty war' in Argentina).

In the second part (contextualization) we will dare to ask what this
text means to us Christians now. The sovereign God works and
responds in our human predicaments, no matter how violent, sinful,

desperate it may be at the end of the second millennium. The Holy Spirit is with us, among us; not retired somewhere else in the cosmos.

I. Historical-literary context

The Books of Samuel present the radical transformation that occurred in the life of Ancient Israel when Israel ceased to be a marginal company of tribes and became a centralized state[1].

I Samuel 1–3 traces the birth and life of one who became a leader of Yahweh, a prophet and a religious and civic figure, a key person in all this new stage of development.

Israel in those days was a marginal community through the power and pressure of the Philistines. It was economically, politically and socially weak. Also, at the end of the book of Judges it is portrayed as a society of moral chaos, engaged in gross brutality. Waiting for God's deliverance and liberation was fraught with bitterness.

Born of a humble and powerless family (like so many key biblical figures, e.g. the disciples of Jesus), a single Ephraimite family, a mother who is cursed according to that culture because she was barren, Hannah prays in the midst of desperation and faith, depression and grief, hope and waiting, a waiting which starts in apparent hopelessness and ends in victory. God's almighty purposes for Israel are revealed and given in answer to her prayer.

Let us recall that Hannah has been laughed at, scorned and abused by Peninnah (I Sam. 4–6), the other wife of Elkanah, who has borne him children. Her own beloved husband has not understood the depth of her grief, and even the priest of the temple, Eli, judged her wrongly in her prayer and accused her of being drunk. She was not drunk in prayer, but rather mumbling a desperate plea to God in which she vowed that the fruit of her womb would be dedicated to God's service and will. Certainly God responded and Samuel became a champion of Jewish faith, a prophet and a religious and civic leader.

We can understand her despair, because in those days people were convinced that sterility was a judgment of God upon women for past sins. So she felt rejected by God and thus suffered immensely. This rejection must have been felt by Sarah (Gen. 11.30; 15.2; 16.1; 17.12), by Rebecca (Gen. 25.25), by Rachel (Gen. 29.31), by the mother of Samson (Judg. 13.8) and by John the Baptist's mother (Luke 1.7).

The problem of Hannah is resolved by God. It springs from deep faith, hope, love and praise to the Almighty. 'Worship, confident prayer, opens a door to human history and future . . . For those like Hannah (which means "grace") . . .grieved, barren and lonely, God turns barrenness to birth, vexation to praise, isolation to community and worship . . . The narrative is a witness to Yahweh's power, which creates a new historical possibility where none existed. A sovereign will overrides Israel's chaos, to a comfort that overcomes Israel's bitterness . . . it creates a newness of life out of despair . . .'[2]

The text of Hannah (I Sam.2–10) sums up the spirituality of the Old Testament, especially of women. The whole Bible underlies it as its kerygma: God's will to communicate and give of himself to humankind. It is human faith and God's answer in dialectical action, the outcome of his faithfulness and of human praise for it. Gerhard von Rad explains that the whole 'redeeming event' between God and his people is summed up in promise-fulfilment. It is the spirituality of the *Shema*: 'Hear, Israel, Yahweh is our God and He is one' (Deut. 6.4).

The songs of women in the Old and New Testaments represent their faith and the Lord's answer, ending in prophetic vision and praise. The song we are studying is considered the first *Magnificat*, very much like Mary's in the New Testament (Luke 1.44–55).

One of the oldest examples of psalm compositions is Deborah's song in the book of Judges, a masterpiece of Hebrew literature written certainly under the immediate impact of God's actions (Judg. 5.1ff.). The attitude of praise before God's actions and promises of deliverance-liberation characterize the deep spirituality of women portrayed in the whole Bible. The song of Miriam, prophet, sister of Moses and Aaron (Ex. 15.1–21), is another feminine response. She led the men and women in praise, song and dance for God's mighty acts in the history of their liberation. Judith is another similar answer of thanksgiving for God's action for the people (Judith 16.1ff.). This is a psalm hymn like Mary's and Hannah's 'Magnificat'. In ch. 13 Ozias' exclamation to Judith is repeated again by Elizabeth to Mary in her greeting (Luke 1.42; cf. Judith 13.18–20).

From historical and literary analysis we can conclude that in the biblical tradition there is a significant strain of psalmodic-prophetic songs of women, a symbol of human response, full of faith and love to the global, divine mystery of God's intervention. God is mighty to those who, due to their historical, social, cultural and political situations, are conscious of their own helplessness; those who have no access to power or ability to effect change.

The main theological themes in Hannah's song (cf. Mary's *Magnificat*) are:

1. Acknowledgment of God's power to transform concrete situations of oppression on behalf of the powerless. 'My heart, my strength, my mouth, my enemies' (v. 1 is in contrast to 'your deliverance'). It is her joy and God's power of liberation. The hope and assurance is that Yahweh is the

One who has the power to transform and willingness to intervene on behalf of the powerless. If we believe in his willingness to intervene without utter trust in his power to transform we fall finally into pitiful sentimentality.

2. The reversal of the full and the hungry, the barren and the fruitful, by Yahweh's intervention changes the disproportion of power and potentiality in human transactions (cf. Luke 16.19–31). Such an 'irrational' hope is an act of faith that all of God's gifts have not already been committed to present social, political, cultural arrangements. God has powerful gifts for the marginal. In v. 8 we can clearly see the 'dangerous' social implications of 'a resurrection to faith'. One can imagine the haughtiness of Peninnah (1.4–6), who seemed so privileged. One can imagine the arrogance of the Philistines, who seemed so secure. Later one can sense (and resent) the pride of Babylon, who seemed ordained to dominate the world for ever (Isa 47.1–2). The world belongs to Yahweh because he created it, redeemed it and sustains it (cf. Deut. 10.14, 17–18). The hope of the weak is rooted in the power of their Creator and Redeemer. Arrogant human strength cannot prevail.

3. Long before Saul and David or any king that appeared in Israel, the psalm of Hannah asserts that the coming king (the Messiah) will be the agent of the poor, the needy, the hungry, the barren (cf. Ps. 72.1–4, 12–14). This poem speaks of a future beyond Hannah's future, already enunciating the signs of Christ's kingdom.

In summary, consider these words of Walter Brueggemann:

> This song becomes the Song of Mary and the Song of the Church (Luke 1.46–55), as the faithful community finds in Jesus the means through which Yahweh will turn and right the world. The Song of Mary, derived from Hannah, becomes the source for Luke's radical portrayal of Jesus. This song becomes a source of deep and dangerous hope in the world wherever the prospect and possibility of human arrangements have been exhausted. When people can no longer believe the promises of the rules of this age, when the gifts of well-being are no longer given through established channels, this song voices an alternative to which the desperate faithful cling.
>
> Our interpretative responsibility now is to see who among us can join this dangerous, daring song to this same God who has power to transform and willingness to intervene.[3]

We dare not forget that the beauty and depth of these passages and of the women's lives that give them concrete human (and also divine!) validity make up a composite package from which we cannot remove any part without seriously endangering the whole. They grow out of moving mystical experiences of a living God. They bear unshakable testimony to

God's sovereignty over all our personal life and over all our life together in society on his planet. They move with utter inevitability and naturalness into politics, 'international' relations, power, culture, even to the eternally recurring problem of war and peace.

II. Contextualization

Just a few years before the third millennium we live in a world in which there are wars (cf. Rwanda, Croatia, etc.); religious fanaticism (the bombing of AMIA – the Israeli Association of Mutual Assistance in Buenos Aires); more recently Oklahoma, USA; death by sub-human conditions (three-quarters of the world); AIDS, another kind of brutality spreading fast all over the world (where society kills people by ostracism before their final death); warehouses full of the mentally retarded, of old people, of young delinquents, collections of children (for sale in Chile, Argentina and Paraguay). There are children for markets in Europe and the USA – some to be adopted, others to be used in begging and prostitution (especially young girls) or in organ transplants. Sheer madness creates pseudo-religions that kill thousands (Japan/Waco, Texas). Gurus take the place of a God of justice and life; cults of all sorts demand human sacrifice of babies and adults; sorcery, witches (men and women) that promise and demand fanaticism, racism, sexism; the ecological devastation of our planet by the lust for power for the sake of power, political and social corruption are only examples of today's degeneration on a global scale.

In this kind of world of 'terrorisms' of every sort of God's mighty justice, love and care seem utter illusion, and scepticism prevails in young and old. People seek answers out of utter desperation for mere physical and psychological survival. The whole creation is either in 'birth pains' ending in apocalyptic monstrosities or lives in a 'hope against hope' (Rom 4.18–21), which is born of faith and costly grace (not cheap grace, cf. Dietrich Bonhoeffer, *The Cost of Discipleship*).

We certainly live in a time of deep crisis for the whole Christian church, a church that should be in the 'diaspora', as Richard Shaull pointed out many years ago, right there where people's needs are met, and not enclosed in a temple on Sundays, only to 'give people a life' as believers watch history from the balcony, as John Mackay said and wrote half a century ago.

This very moment of history demands a renewal of Christian faith, full of hope and love for our neighbour, especially the oppressed, the voiceless, the helpless and all creatures, including animals and plants that cannot defend themselves or demand their God-given rights. It demands a faith which is not confused with sentimental withdrawal from people's real problems (political-social-cultural) and does not take the attitude of the overwhelming majority: 'Count me out, I just can't do anything!' Certainly, we cannot reverse many situations, but God is sovereign in our insecurities and God can! Certainly God can if we are ready to follow the paths of the kingdom together with the so-called non-persons (G. Gutiérrez), the voiceless, the dispossessed. Jesus spoke in the Beatitudes to these people and to all who follow our Creator and Redeemer with the faith, courage, hope and love of Hannah, Elizabeth or Mary or the women and men who are disciples of all ages.

'Hope against hope' is to receive by faith the promises of life abundant for all, not just for a few privileged ones who decide on other people's life or death. We are surrounded by literal holocausts (cf. the Argentine 'dirty war', now after years of silence confessed by our army's chief general: the assassination of thousands of men, women and children, tortured in concentration camps by army, police, para-police – our own SS!). Life abundant means salvation or liberation for humanity and creation as a whole.

To hope like Hannah is already to have a new future opened in spite of failures, suffering, humiliations, threats, disillusionment. Faith without hope may create hatred and vengeance; nurtured by hope, it may create new communities of prophetic voices that denounce structural sins and announce the good news of the kerygma.

Hannah's faith and hope, like our hope and faith, are not produced by us. They are not a psychological phenomenon to keep us going in spite of desperate situations. If the Christian *waits* on the liberation from oppressive, dehumanizing, annihilating events, it is not because she/he needs to survive.

Of course there is a crisis of hope among all (Christians and non-Christians). When we are well-fed, have an income adequate to live with dignity, have a sheltering roof under which to sleep, we do not need to exercise faith or hope. In dialectical tension Christian faith-hope-love and God's response do not depend on temporary feelings; it is not offered as a vague, soothing solution that may be a veiled form of escapism. It is not cheap grace but costly grace. As I have said, it offers God's intervening action of liberation, healing, community-forming life in every sense, to be enjoyed, not endured. We do not create it, we receive it, if we ask in humble prayer and praise in the midst of our suffering and helplessness. God responds. God acts. It is a matter of waiting, like Hannah, for God's future. It is only illusion when we try to work alone without God and without loving others.

If the pain of our world does not hurt us, we do not love God or our neighbour; the biblical paradox is that Christian hope really means total insecurity opening up to total security. It does not stand on what we have at our disposal, nor does it fall before our limited visions and pretensions. As God himself is the giver, it is more assurance than any human certitude. He is faithful; all rests on God's faithfulness and his promises. This thus liberates us from pessimism and also from false optimism. It never ceases, is always open to a new future.

Faith and hope sustain each other, as in Hannah's prayer the praying and the singing do. They are intimately related to God; that is why we are to give our best to the Lord and wait for his response – a waiting which is not only for oneself but also for others, especially an eager longing for the accomplishment of God's almighty purposes.

This kind of faith-hope-love-praise refuses to leave any other human being to a fatal destiny. The Talmud says that 'to save one life is to save humanity'. It is impossible to follow Christ without loving him concretely, with incarnate love that stands beside the poor, the dispossessed, the oppressed and lives in service to God and to others. From this life-style springs the deep spirituality revealed in the characters of the Bible and in Christians all through the ages. From this kind of living springs God's liberation and true human joy and life!

Let me close with one of the thoughts recorded in her own handwriting and bequeathed to me by the late Ana Maria Melano, my only sister – a Hannah of the twentieth century, whose faith and love were more than unusual:

Love and do as you please. If you keep silence, you will keep in love. If you correct, it will be correction in love. If you forgive, you will forgive in love. If inside you there is the root of love, nothing but goodness can spring from that root.

Amen.

Notes

1. Walter Brueggemann. *First and Second Samuel*, Interpretation. A Bible Commentary for Teaching and Preaching, Louisville 1990, 10–21.
2. Ibid., 12.
3. Ibid., 21.

Beyond the Market: The Growth of the Informal Economy

Gregory Baum

The globalization of the economy

The globalization of the free-market economy is at present transforming the industrial societies of the West. In North America this process has gone very far. The power to control the national life is gradually moving from national governments to transnational corporations. To forestall the flight of the industries, national governments are obliged to create advantageous conditions for the industries and exempt them from taxation. National governments, forced to orientate the economic development of their country on international competitivity, are becoming unable to protect the material well-being of their citizens. Because the tax base has shifted from the corporation and the wealthy to the middle classes (as well as for other reasons), governments have become indebted and are thus obliged to economize, yet they lack the power to ensure that the financial burden is distributed in society in accordance with principles of justice. The sacrifice is imposed on the weakest members of society and on institutions that do not serve the goal of international competitiveness. 'Down-sizing' is becoming the key word not only for the public but also for the private sector. The new electronic technology, which made the globalization of the economy possible, also allows banks, commercial companies and industries of various kinds to replace a growing number of workers and employees by sophisticated automated machinery.

The 'clover leaf' society

These changes are creating in society a widening sector of people at the margin, often called 'the third sector', constituted by the unemployed and men and women on welfare as well as people who are precariously employed, have a part-time job, or are so poorly paid that they cannot support their families. This sector is not likely to shrink. For even if there should be a return to industrial growth, the economic recovery will be jobless. Thanks to the technology, we do not need all these people. The production of wealth can proceed without them.

Contemporary society increasingly resembles a clover leaf with three lobes or sectors, where 'the first sector' embraces the economic and political elites and the professionals working for them, 'the second sector' includes salaried people and organized workers with secure jobs and a decent income, and 'the third sector' is constituted by the marginalized. I shall follow this terminology in the present article.

Several years ago the American economist John Kenneth Galbraith designated as 'the contented majority' the people whose needs are fulfilled by the American economy[1] – in our terminology the first and second sector of the clover-leaf society. According to Galbraith, this majority, about 70% at the time of his writing, remains indifferent to the suffering of the men, women and children belonging to the third sector; and since the majority holds power in a democracy, it is able to keep the system from changing. Since at this time the second sector is shrinking while the third sector expands, one begins to wonder how long 'the contented' will remain the majority.

Community development

Something of great importance is happening in the third or marginal sector of all Western capitalist countries. Men and women, refusing to remain passive, and inspired by persons with leadership talent, have created major interlocking networks of self-help organizations that have political, economic and social significance. Some of these organizations have a political purpose: they try to exert pressure on governments or corporations to protect their neighbourhood, their region or their nation. An example of this is the Canada Action Network, originally organized to oppose the Free Trade Agreement with the United States, that continues to promote an alternative vision of Canadian society. Other self-help organizations, many of them quite small, have an economic purpose: they deal with local needs by setting up neighbourhood co-operatives, loan associations, collectively run stores, common kitchens, home repair shops, joint backyard food production, and many other activities. Other self-help organizations have a social purpose: these include day-care services, shelters for battered women, rescue from substance abuse, houses for refugees, training centres, popular education, and store-front offices for counselling recent immigrants and refugees.[2]

All of these associations have an important social and cultural role, even if their main purpose should be political or economic. They rescue people from their isolation, they stir up their energies, they lead them to action, and they create community. This movement is often called 'community development'.[3]

Since the larger projects of community development are in need of a few full-time, salaried facilitators, they must find some financial support from outside sources: national, provincial or municipal governments, chartered foundations, corporations, community loan funds, credit unions and other publicly-minded institutions, including churches and synagogues. The other portion of their support comes from the small fees paid by their clients and, more especially, from the work done by the volunteers, including people drawn from the middle classes. Volunteer labour is indispensable.

It is characteristic of community development that its activities correspond to the socio-economic and cultural needs defined by the local community. The decisions about its operations are made in a dialogue involving the clients and the people (paid and unpaid) who offer the help. This process is often called 'social learning'. The democratic interaction among clients and workers makes community development different from publicly-funded welfare organizations and privately-run capitalist institutions. Community development is a challenging enterprise because it involves the co-operation of paid and unpaid persons with different educational backgrounds and belonging to different economic classes. This demands great skill on the part of the facilitators and great virtue on the part of all participants. Joint projects begun with great enthusiasm sometimes fail because of tensions and misunderstandings. On the other hand, if the co-operation suceeds, the activities create a strong sense of social solidarity in all the participants, a counter-cultural mentality at odds with the capitalist mind-set.

The larger projects of community development create some jobs, low-paying jobs for the most part. In some cases, governments support community development as a strategy for creating employment. This support is gladly accepted as long as government does not try to control the initiatives of the local community.

The informal economy

The economic dimension of community development deserves special attention. If 'the formal economy' refers to the registered and taxed economic activity constituting the Gross National Product, the economic activity of community development can be largely associated with 'the informal economy', operating outside the market, consisting mainly of volunteering, reciprocity, exchange and householding. Mainstream economists tend to neglect the informal economy, even though no society can survive without it. Even in capitalist society, services rendered freely or in exchange for services received have always been present in the family, among friends, and in poorer neighbourhoods and regions. Community development can be looked upon as an explosion of the informal economy: only when it creates jobs, low-paid though they be, does it re-enter the market.

According to the economic historian Karl Polanyi, in pre-capitalist society economic activity was embedded in people's social relations and strengthened the commonly shared social bond. The earliest economic activities were reciprocity, redistribution, exchange and householding. Markets for buying and selling of commodities developed much later. Even when markets assumed greater importance, the great majority of people lived from labour in its traditional forms. In *The Great Trans-formation*,[4] Karl Polanyi has shown that the characteristic of the capitalist organization of labour was that it separated workers and employees from the community to which they belonged and failed to create new social bonds among them and their families. Industrial capitalism 'disembedded' people's economic activity from the web of their social relations, a process which, according to Polanyi, produced isolation, cultural loss and the breakdown of solidarity. Economic poverty, Polanyi argued, is not a tragedy if the people belong to a community with self-help skills and a strong sense of solidarity: this, after all, is how most of humanity has lived through its history. But economic poverty is devastating and soul-destroying if people do *not* belong to such a community. The great harm done by industrial capitalism is the production of social disintegration. The healing of modern society, Polanyi argued, will not take place through economic growth, nor even through a more just distribution of wealth, however important this may be, but through the 're-embedding' of economic activity in the life of the community, creating social solidarity and a culture of co-operation.

One of the theses of *The Great Transformation* is that the self-regulating market system, deeply at odds with all previous human experience, summons forth a counter-movement in society, especially at the base, that tries to protect community, foster co-operation, and preserve the land. A significant number of scholars have interpreted community development as an instance of this counter-movement: a return to reciprocity and volunteering, a re-embedding of economic activity in social relations, a creation of co-operative culture.[5] Since in many instances community development creates some paid employment and therefore moves into the formal economy, some authors refer to community development as 'the social economy', stressing the social bond created by the economic activity.

Are there reasons to be sceptical?

Community development touches a minority of people in society. In fact, people who have no personal relation to it are not even aware that it exists, even if many small community projects operate in their own neighbourhood. Yet community development has attracted the attention of social scientists. Studies on these activities abound. Several years ago a congress held at Montreal brought together scholars from Europe and North America to report on and evaluate the spread of community development in their countries.[6] Most participants interpreted the spread of the social economy as a creative response to chronic unemployment and the decline of the welfare state, a response that had wider social significance.

There were also negative voices. Some social scientists drew attention to the degree of personal dedication required from the facilitators, causing many of them to be completely exhausted after a few years. They called community development the self-exploitation of the poor. Others suggested that governments offered support for community projects because it kept the people in poor neighbourhoods working, tamed them, and kept them from organizing political protest.

Another problem is the following. Because in many instances the new social movement creates a good number of low-paying jobs, certain governments look upon it with favour and even suggest that, if adequately supported, it could be the solution for the entire problem of unemployment. Some community leaders protest against this.[7] They see community development as a creative strategy in the low-income sectors of society, as a good idea in a bad situation. They are afraid, therefore, that instead of stimulating industrial development, retraining workers for new tasks and creating decently-paid jobs in the mainstream economy, governments may think of the future in terms of community development and low-paying, low-skilled, precarious jobs for the majority of working people. If community development became a major item of government policy, the social economy would cease to be a self-determining, community-based, self-help enterprise.

Another abuse of community development is the introduction of 'workfare', forcing welfare recipients to work for the community in jobs assigned to them by government. Apart from the contradiction between 'workfare' and democratic theory, obliging people to participate in community development would undermine its spirit and its principle of organization.

These are the reasons why some observers of community development emphasize its precarious character, threatened either by the excessive demands made on the participants or by the effort of government to control and use it for its own purpose.

The wider social significance

By contrast, many students of community development regard it as a movement of important social significance, that is to say not only as serving the well-being of masses of unemployed and otherwise excluded people, but also as being a stepping-stone towards the transformation of society. Here we find two different views.

According to one view, community development is a creative movement in the marginal sector that helps vast numbers of people, but is unable to overcome the division of society between those who have access to power and wealth and those who are excluded from them. Yet since in every country engagement in the social economy creates a culture of co-operation and solidarity at odds with capitalist values, community development may eventually lay the foundation for a new, mass-based, international political movement inspired by a vision of an alternative society, ready to tame the international market.[8]

An alternative view sees community development among the marginalized as part of the so-called voluntary sector, constituted by the more traditional non-profit organizations that employ a professional staff, rely on financial support from governments and other donors, and depend upon volunteers for their full operation. Non-profit organizations offer cultural, educational, health and counselling services to people of all classes: they are not located in the marginal class. As governments are cutting support for welfare, these non-profit organizations are destined to play a larger role in society and for this reason appeal to the public for stronger support and greater voluntary participation. Since the word 'volunteering' tends to suggest charity, old-fashioned virtue and conservative ideology, the non-profit organizations are looking for an alternative terminology. They see volunteering in non-profit organizations and community development as a critical, society-transforming activity. Some social thinkers believe that as men and women become mobilized as active, participating citizens, the voluntary sector including community development will be able to offer people the material goods they need and the cultural goods they want, thus replacing the highly inflexible and bureaucratized welfare state.[9] If public money supports the infrastructure of these community enterprises and if citizens involve themselves in providing these services, society will become more participatory, more de-centralized, and more adaptable to the needs of local communities. From this perspective, community development appears as a training ground for the practice of active citizenship.

Notes

1. Cf. John Kenneth Galbraith, *The Culture of Contentment*, Boston 1992.
2. Each country has its own literature. For developments in the USA, see Harry Boyte, *The Backyard Revolution*, Philadelphia 1980; Severyn Bruins and James Meehen, *Beyond the Market and the State: New Directions in Community Development*, 1987; Meredith Ramsey, *Community, Culture and Economic Development: The Social Roots of Local Action*, New York 1996. For developments in Canada, see David Ross and Peter Usher, *From the Roots Up: Economic Development as if Community Mattered*, Toronto 1986; Louis Favreau, *Mouvements populaires et interventions communautaires*, Montréal 1989.
3. In Quebec 'community development' is called 'le mouvement communautaire', while in France the preferred term is 'le mouvement associatif'.
4. Karl Polanyi, *The Great Transformation* (1942), published in many editions. See also Gregory Baum, *Karl Polanyi on Ethics and Economics*, Montreal 1996.
5. This position has been defended by several authors in *The Legacy of Karl Polanyi*, ed. Marguerite Mendell and Daniel Salée, New York 1991: among them are the editors, M. Mendell and D. Salée, and Brent McClinton, J. Ron Stanfield, Trent Schroyer and Björn Hettne.
6. For the proceedings, see Benoît Lévesque et al. (ed.), *L'autre économie*, Montreal 1989.
7. Because of overtures made by the Quebec government, the issue is hotly debated in Quebec society. See, for example, Konrad Yakabuski, 'L'économie sociale: rêve ou cauchemar?', in *Le Devoir*, 30 and 31 March 1996, and Jean-Marc Fontan and Éric Shragge, 'L'economie sociale: une économie pour les pauvres?', in *La Presse*, 30 April 1996.
8. This position is argued by the Quebec review, *Virtualités*.
9. See Lester Salamon, *Partners in Public Service*, Baltimore 1995.

II · The Market and Religion

Christianity in the Context of Globalized Capitalistic Markets

Ulrich Duchrow

I. The phases of political economy in the twentieth century

1. The collapse of the global classical liberal system

If we are trying to take our bearings in the complex political and economic scene of today, it is natural to look back at previous phases in this century. It began with the eclipse of the classical liberal system which had been dominated by England. This was based on the belief that economics followed mechanistic laws like those of classical physics. Adam Smith saw himself as the Newton of economics, i.e. its founder as a science. Its laws, he believed, lead to the prosperity of all nations provided that one allows them to work without outside intervention, i.e. intervention by the state. Each strives for riches, and through the absolute competition the selfish agents in the market hold one another in check and advance developments in a way which is favourable for all.

However, the application of this economistic faith did not lead to the prosperity of all, and of all nations. Within the nations the masses became impoverished. Internationally, liberalism led to an intensification of colonialism on the one hand and the competition of the great European imperial powers striving for hegemony on the other. The result was the great world economic crisis of 1929 with its concomitant mass unemployment, great misery and two world wars – all this impressively described by Eric Hobsbawm in his book *The Age of Extremes*.

Essentially three theological positions could be taken on the dogma of classical liberalism. On one side were the theologians who simply reflected and legitimated the liberal development. As long as this went relatively well, the material and moral progress in it was praised (culture

Protestantism). When the crises became clearer at the end of the nineteenth century, people followed Max Weber in adopting the thesis of the 'autonomy of spheres of life' with which the harshness of the system and the warlike elements in the competitive system could readily be legitimated (the late Friedrich Naumann). The obverse of this position is the restriction of what is really Christian to the person and its inwardness, if need be supplemented by unpolitical charitable activity.

On the other side stood the Religious Socialists, who regarded capitalism as such as incompatible with Christian faith and therefore joined the Workers' Movement in seeking alternatives. A middle position was adopted by those who, like some governments, wanted to prevent existing property-holding from being endangered as a result of strong social antagonisms. Mention should be made here of Pope Leo XIII's famous 1891 encyclical *Rerum novarum*, the basis of later Catholic social teaching.

The great crisis of the early twentieth century led to the cards being reshuffled. Pure, liberal capitalism had run into the ground. It had been global, in the form of the system of the imperial European powers, dominated by England, with gold as a world currency. The counter-reaction to the crisis (or crises) took the form first of attempts to regain national control of the economy.

Granted, the theory of the first group, socialism, was universalistic. Socialism expected the contradictions of capitalism to lead to a universal revolution in the form of socialism and communism – though also following a scientifically recognizable law of history. But in fact the proletarian revolution initially succeeded only in Russia, from which Stalin developed the conception of 'socialism in one country'.

The second form of reaction to the crisis of global liberalism was national capitalism (a better name for Fascism than National Socialism, since it saw socialism along with Christianity as its main opponent). The attacks of Fascist national capitalism were directed against global liberal capitalism in its form dominated by Anglo-Saxon high finance – moreover with a focus on 'world Jewry', which was allegedly in control. Hitler's collaboration with the forces of national capitalism like the Deutsche Bank, Daimler-Benz and IG-Farben is well known.

The most important response to the collapse of classical liberalism for the West was given by the English economist John Maynard Keynes. It determined the policy of nation states until the early 1970s. His proposals for the international economic order, which were only very partially put into practice, are now once again inspiring the quest for alternatives to the neo-liberal globalization of the capitalist world economy. So we must pay particular attention to his view.

2. John Maynard Keynes

Keynes deliberately parted company with belief in the autonomous self-regulation of the market for the good of all. This goal, he argued, can only be attained by conscious political direction. The criteria for such action are justice, equilibrium and peace. Keynes's great theoretical achievement, which he worked out especially in his *General Theory* (1937), consisted in demonstrating that full employment, regular growth and an increase in purchasing power are possible if the state itself guides investment activity in a cycle which runs opposite to the economic situation. If in addition taxation policy damps speculation and progressive taxation of wealth finances social policies, the result can be what we call a welfare state.

The great efficiency of this model is shown by a comparison between the phase influenced by Keynes and the neo-liberal phase: between 1950 and 1978 in the USA the income of the poorest 20% rose by 140%, and that of the richest by 99%; by contrast, between 1978 and 1993 the income of the poorest fell by 19%, while that of the richest increased by 18%.[1]

Keynes also worked out an impressive model in the international context, concerned to achieve equilibrium. This was his plan for the Bretton Woods Conference of 1944, which was to develop the institutions and the policies for a post-war world economy.[2] In connection with the problem of globalization it is important to remember that here Keynes presupposed sovereign nation states also in economic policy, and the international system was to establish the primacy of politics over economics strictly in analogy to the nation states.

The USA for its part put forward the White Plan, which changed essential elements in the Keynes plan – at precisely the points where the original Bretton Woods system later failed and had to give way to the neo-liberal model.[3]

From the perspective of the churches and theology this second phase between the Second World War and the beginning of the 1970s was governed by the founding of the World Council of Churches (WCC) in 1948 and the Second Vatican Council (1962–1965). In this period the social ethic of the WCC was governed by the concept of a 'responsible society', which had been prepared for since 1937. Claiming to discover a third way beyond capitalism and communism, this fitted the Keynesian approach of a nationally and internationally regulated market economy very well. The momentous wrong decisions made at Bretton Woods had not yet been perceived, especially as the political decolonization of the countries of Asia and Africa was at the forefront of attention.

Only in 1966, when at the great Geneva Conference on Church and Society the voices of the South began to shape the agenda, did the fact that the structures of dependence in the world system were also economic begin to emerge. The Second Vatican Council sparked off a similar development in the Roman Catholic Church. Here it was the Conference of Latin American Bishops in Medellin which brought the biblical insight of 'God's option for the poor' into the centre and thus legitimated and reinforced the impressive development towards base communities and liberation theology. The resolutions of Medellin were also seen as an indirect recognition of the armed war of liberation. The USA responded to this development with Low Intensity Conflict Strategy (LIC), sometimes hand in hand with the Curia in Rome.[4]

To sum up, it can be said that the post-war interest of the excessively powerful USA in opening up the way all over the world for its big businesses and its dollars increasingly led to the freeing of economic forces from political control and direction. On the transnational globalized markets the socially divisive and exclusive competition to maximize profits and reduce costs, which is also destructive of the environment, could begin its course unrestricted. By contrast, liberation from unjust structures of dependence did not get beyond its initial successes in the political sphere. The take-over of power by capitalist forces which were acting in an area with fewer and fewer barriers could not be slowed down. From an ideological perspective, however, this period saw the rise of liberation theology, which meanwhile had come to have a world-wide influence and in church history represents an epoch-making shift from Constantinian Christianity to being the people of God, with a biblical orientation.

3. The neo-liberal phase of the globalization of economic power

In 1975 the German Federal Chancellor Helmut Schmidt and the French President Giscard d'Estaing organized a first meeting of the heads of state of the seven richest industrial nations, first of all for informal discussions about the changed situation. From this arose the annual 'economic summits' of the G7 countries. After initial attempts at regulation coming from Social Democrats, when Reagan took power in the USA, Thatcher in Britain and Kohl in Germany, the group of the seven richest industrial countries embarked fully on the course of liberalization. The most recent summit in Lyons in 1996 once again expressed at length the dogma of free trade, privatization and deregulated markets.[5] Although by now everyone is aware that in present conditions economic growth does not create employment but destroys it (because the profits are invested in rationalization), this dogma is also being proclaimed again. It must therefore be clearly emphasized that while the development from a socially-regulated market economy to pure globalized capitalism may be economically induced, it is politically tolerated and even pursued, and therefore must be responded to. The three great economic powers, USA, Japan and Germany, bear the main responsibility for this.

Meanwhile an extensive literature about individual problem spheres has developed.[6] Here I only want to emphasize two elements which play a fundamental role in Keynes and which therefore help us to understand the changed situation: employment and the role of the state.

Technical innovations, particularly in data-processing, mean that the work that needs to be done is indisputably less. The response to this in principle could be that the smaller amount of work is distributed fairly and everyone works shorter hours. In principle the increases in productivity could also be distributed in such a way that the real incomes of the workers and thus their living standard are preserved or, in the poorer regions, improved. But instead of this, the transnational corporations produce unemployment in order at the same time to put pressure on the wages of those who still have work. In addition to exploiting the dependent work-force, this also excludes an increasing number of people from the formal economy. That again deprives the state of taxes from the income which depends on this and at the same time burdens the budget with additional costs to finance the unemployed.

Not content with this, capital uses the free capital markets to avoid tax gains. That comes about through manipulations of transfer prices in the real economy, but above all through monetary transactions in tax havens. The result is that even in the rich industrial nations budgets go into deficit. The deficit in public budgets in turn serves as a lever for capital to compel states to 'structural adaptation programmes'. The International Monetary Fund and the World Bank have long been getting a grip on the debtor countries of the South. They give absolute priority to payment of interest to creditors. These programmes involve reductions in state expenditure, and that becomes a burden on social, education and health programmes. They force wages down and give capital every possibility of increasing profit through deregulation and privatization.

In Europe the same mechanism is enforced through the criteria of convergence towards monetary union. As the state budget can only be in deficit to 60% of Gross Domestic Product (and 3% in respect of new annual indebtedness), it has to save. And where does it do this? Among the poor. Thus the welfare state is dismantled. At the same time the nation states are involved in a competitive safeguarding of their position, i.e. reducing labour and social costs – so that the profits of capital can explode even more.

Only small minorities in the churches and theology of the North have perceived what has happened with the change from the socially-regulated market economy to globalized neo-liberalism. Certainly there was an outcry when the force of social demolition hit individual countries. A few years after Margaret Thatcher took power, the Church of England produced its *Faith in the City* report.[7] Similarly, the Catholic bishops and the United Church of Christ protested after Reagan's policy began to be implemented.[8] Finally, in Germany a consultation process 'On the Economic and Social Situation in Germany' was only introduced in 1994.[9]

Characteristic of all these standpoints is that they complain about the symptoms and call upon their national governments for social action. But apart from some beginnings in the United Church of Christ document, none of these statements analyses the structural change from a nationally-regulated market economy to a deregulated global capitalism. The 'Letter on the Economy' by Dutch groups and organizations and the WCC study text *Christian Faith and the World Economy Today*[10] go furthest here.

Only Latin American bishops and theologians address openly the totalitarian character of the world markets, which are no longer regulated democratically, and the Bretton Woods system controlled by the governments of the rich countries. The works by Franz Hinkelammert on the total market are important here.[11]

II. A biblical theological assessment of the neo-liberal system and possible strategies of resistance

In view of this situation, it does not seem to me to make sense to begin from the traditional method of establishing general theological and ethical principles and then to 'apply' them. Rather, I shall begin from the biblical narratives, each of which in a specific context of social history expresses the basic theological impulse of the various traditions of scripture.[12] Summed up briefly, they produce the following picture:

- In the phase before Israel became a state (c. 1250–1000 BCE) there is a 'national' alternative to the ancient Near Eastern monarchies and empires built up on slavery and tribute.
- In the monarchy (1000–586 BCE) the monarchical system, which is intrinsically questionable for Israel, is tamed by the prophetic criticism of power and law, orientated on justice and peace.
- In the exilic and Persian periods (586–533 BCE) there is considerable new reflection on the question: how can Israel nevertheless live in accordance with the life-giving commandments of its God in the niche of a world empire?
- In the period of the totalitarian Hellenistic-Roman empires, all that was left was resistance in various forms and hope for the kingdom of God with a human face that would overcome the world empires. With Jesus and his movement there is also the powerful conviction that even

in these circumstances the kingdom of God already creates alternatives in the microcosm through small messianic cells.

In all these phases the basic conviction prevails that the question of God is an issue in political, economic and ideological questions. What functions as an absolute, as God, in a society? How can these approaches be applied today in a situation in which there are both niches and elements which can be influenced by prophecy and law, as well as a totalitarian overall framework?

1. Why there can be no going back behind Keynes

If one wants to find a name for the move from a market economy orientated on social justice and an international equilibrium in the Keynesian sense to globalized neo-liberalism, a first approach would be to say that the Keynesian national regulation of market forces collapsed because it did not succeed in establishing its international political system of regulation at Bretton Woods in the face of the United States. The unfettered transnational capitalist markets shattered even the national instruments of regulation from the outside.

That will be the reason why departments of the United Nations Organization like the United Nations Development Programme, the European Community Commission/FAST programme and non-governmental organizations like the Transnational Institute are taking up Keynes's Bretton Woods proposals again.[13] In the framework of the United Nations Organization these include a World Economic Security Council to which even the Bretton Woods institutions, which would be democratized, would be accountable. The International Monetary Fund would become a World Central Bank. Its special drawing rights would be developed into an international Special Bank Fund. This would among other things be financed by global taxation on speculative activity (Tobin tax), on income and energy expenditure, and on the 'peace dividend' (savings from disarmament). The world trade system would be given, as Keynes envisaged, a better mechanism for stabilizing raw material prices, and sociological and ecological support, including an international environment tax. The flight from taxation would be stemmed by the taxation of tax havens. The non-governmental organizations would have a legitimate place within all global tax institutions as representatives of the citizens of the world who are affected.

There can be no doubt that the implementation of these measures would result in a revolutionary improvement in the living conditions of all men and women. But all previous attempts to put them on the international agenda, e.g. at the world social summit in Copenhagen in 1995, have failed. The governments of the industrialized countries blocked all the efforts of the United Nations and the non-governmental organizations in this direction.

In addition, at least two basic elements of the Keynesian solutions no longer function. The presupposition of the first is that investment is equal to employment, which is why one of the prime functions of the state in economic policy is to influence investment activity by moving in the opposite direction from it. But in the meantime businesses are investing in rationalization, i.e. cutting down employment. So here there is need of a further taxation element – but now international: namely, a mechanism which ensures that gains in productivity are accompanied by reductions in working hours, not the abolition of jobs. That could come about, for example, through a (global) alteration to the taxation system according to which it was no longer labour but machines and using up the environment that were taxed. So here there would be ways of implementing Keynes's concern for full employment in changed circumstances – if the political will was there.

A second point is far more difficult: Keynes expected unlimited possibilities of economic growth. This is ecologically no longer tolerable. H. C. Binswanger has pointed out that the compulsion to growth in the economy follows from the nature of the modern money economy.[14] There can be no nil growth with this kind of monetary mechanism.

That brings us to the theroetical limits to Keynes. He has not noted what Aristotle already reflected on in the face of the rising money economy and Marx reflected on under the conditions of mature capitalism: in principle there are two forms of economy.[15] One is orientated on the satisfaction of particular needs. It knows trade in the form of barter (in which money can serve as a means of exchange). The other form is orientated on the abstract idea of the increase of money. Aristotle sees it as an illusion that human beings in their greed think that they can buy an infinite amount of resources with money; precisely in so doing they destroy 'the good life', i.e. 'life in community'. Through a formula for calculating interest which even leaves out the material part of the production, circulation and consumption of commodities, the illusion becomes perfect: money itself seems to generate more money. Marx calls this 'capital fetishism', and in so doing hits on the religious character of the capitalist system. Pure capitalism functions only in accordance with this mechanism of the increase of wealth, and knows human beings and nature only as costs, not as concrete life; it therefore thoughtlessly destroys them. It is anethical, not unethical, as Max Weber put it. The pure mechanism of the capitalistic markets is 'slavery without a master'.[16]

So the establishment of purely capitalistic world markets with their agents and institutions is to be rejected in principle, not only for ecological and social but also for theological reasons. Pure increase of money at the cost of life is an idol, mammon. This clear No is being said today by a majority only among church governments and theologians from Asia, Africa and Latin America. In the North only a tiny majority are in favour of it. Furthermore growing Neo-Pentecostalist, charismatic and fundamentalist groups reflect the reality of the market in various ways and even provide ideological support for it. On the one hand, the masses which are becoming increasingly impoverished look to these groups for comfort. On the other, market forces (and in part also the CIA, as in Guatemala) use this religious feeling to put religion at the service of capitalist ideology and interests. That is the reason why sometimes enormous sums of money are put at the disposal of these groups for their electronic media. It is of great significance for committed Christians, base communities and churches to enter into dialogue with those who are being led astray by these groups, and to develop common perspectives of action with them in the light of biblical faith.

Given the totalization of the capitalist money economy and today's ecological insights, the mechanism and fetishism of capital is itself coming into view, a perception of which takes us beyond Keynes.

2. Economies orientated on need from below bound up with political regulation – a double strategy

For Jesus, a clear No is bound up with an equally clear Yes. God's kingdom begins in your midst (Luke 17.21). It begins in small messianic communities which Jesus describes as salt, light and leaven (Matt. 5.13ff.; 13.33). These alternatives in microcosm show themselves in alternative economic structures, so that there are no poor among them (Acts 2.44ff.; 4.32ff.). Whatever the wider context looks like, one can begin new things from below.

This approach points to a common feature of many alternative schemes for the present economic system: the creation of local economic areas with local markets, which are orientated on need, ecologically sustainable and labour-intensive.[17] The decentralization of the provision of energy with renewable sources of energy (sun, wind, water, biomass) and the development of ecological agriculture, best of all in the form of producer-consumer co-operatives, are very important for this development. But what is decisive is control over one's own financial resources – either in credit associations or through a local currency. Barter rings could also be a form of local detachment from the mechanisms of the world market. In short, this first part of a strategy is concerned with the most wide-ranging provision of a region for itself.

However, in the medium term these symbolic alternatives in microcosm must fight for a political framework which deliberately encourages them and at the same time tames the devastating effects of the world market by regulation. Here now all the proposals which Keynes made for national and international political regulation come into play. But without connecting them with a strong local and regional eco-social economy, first the mechanism of capital continues to be dominant, and, secondly, the political will to carry through the political options is not strengthened. Here, moreover, the biblical model of prophetic criticism of power and legal regulations shows its significance and its power. In practice, this approach means that churches and theology today should take part in alliances within civil society and so begin to develop an alternative counter-force. That is the second part of the double strategy, alongside rejection and alternatives in microcosm – in hope for the kingdom of God.

Translated by John Bowden

Notes

1. *Le Monde Diplomatique*, May 1995.
2. Cf. J. K. Horsefield (ed.), *The International Monetary Fund III*, Washington DC 1969, 3ff.
3. Cf. U. Duchrow, *Alternativen zur kapitalistischen Weltwirtschaft. Biblische Erinnerung und politische Ansätze zur Überwindung einer lebensbedrohenden Ökonomie*, Gütersloh 1994, 66ff.
4. Cf. U. Duchrow, G. Eisenbürger and J. Hippler (eds.), *Totaler Krieg gegen die Armen. Geheime Strategiepapiere der amerikanischen Militärs*, Munich ²1991.
5. A single not uninteresting detail deviates from the normal rite: the complaint that the transnational economic forces avoid tax. For more on this see below.
6. The literature up to 1993 is listed in Duchrow, *Alternativen zur kapitalistischen Weltwirtschaft* (n. 3). Cf. recently D. C. Korten, *When Corporations Rule the World*, San Francisco 1995.
7. *Faith in the City*, London 1995.
8. Cf. the 1987 Pastoral Letter of the Catholic Conference of Bishops in the USA, *Justice for All*, and the United Church of Christ's *Christian Faith: Economic Life and Justice. A Pronouncement from the 17th General Synod*, New York 1989.
9. EKD Deutsche Bischofskonferenz, *Zur wirtschaftlichen und sozialen Lage in Deutschland* (1994).
10. 'De keerzijde van der economische Medaille – Een geloofsbrief over de economie', Stuurgroep Project Geloof en Economie (Noordermarkt 26, NL – 1015 Amsterdam) 1992; World Council of Churches, *Christian Faith and the World Economy Today: A Study Document from the WCC*, Geneva 1992.
11. F. J. Hinkelammert, *The Ideological Weapons of Death: A Theological Critique of Capitalism*, Maryknoll 1986.
12. I have described this approach at length in my *Alternativen zur kapitalistischen Weltwirtschaft* (n. 3), and *Versöhnung im Kontext von Nicht-Versöhnung*, supplement to *Junge Kirche* 3/1996, Bremen.

13. For details and bibliography see my *Alternativen zur kapitalistischen Weltwirt-schaft* (n. 3), 276ff.

14. Cf. H. C. Binzwanger, *Geld und Wachstum*, Stuttgart 1994.

15. Cf. Duchrow, *Alternativen zur kapitalistischen Weltwirtschaft* (n. 3), 32ff.

16. Cf. ibid., 113.

17. Cf. Duchrow, *Alternativen zur kapitalistischen Weltwirtschaft* (n. 3), 229 ff., 289f., and further literature, most recently Korten, *When Corporations Rule the World* (n. 6).

Religion, Subjectivity and the Market in Cuba

François Houtart

Introduction

The economic changes being experienced in various countries that either have had or still have a socialist political regime owing to the introduction of a market economy, or elements of this, are having a major impact on their social structures and are also bringing in new cultural elements and social problems. In this new context religions play an ambivalent role. On the one hand, they can contribute to the reconstruction of the necessary ethic, or at least add an element of protection in resolving the new problems of a competitive society. On the other, the churches can either play an accompanying role in the new situation, or they can fall into the temptation of trying to build a new social and political power for themselves, by means of a moral hegemony.

My concern in this article is mainly methodological. How should we analyse these phenomena in sociology and particularly in the sociology of religion? In effect, we have seen not only the fall of the Berlin Wall, the disappearance of the Soviet Union and the break-up of the Eastern bloc, but also – some social scientists claim – the fall of modernity in the sphere of understanding: that is, the loss of a type of understanding that previously enjoyed general acceptance. So we have to take account not only of new facts in such a society as that of Cuba, but also of the whole system of interpreting and ultimately of understanding these facts.

I. The emergence of subjectivity in Cuban society and its incidence on the religious factor

I cannot analyse in detail here what is happening in Cuban society, which would require a more elaborate analytical apparatus, but it is possible to put forward some hypotheses to guide an investigative study. That is what I propose here.

1. Religious phenomena and their interpretation

In Cuba, as in many other societies such as those of former countries of the Soviet Union, and also Vietnam, we are witnessing something of a resurgence of religions. This is too broad a phenomenon to be considered particular to Cuban society alone. It means that there have to be wider grounds for an explanation than those applicable to Cuba on its own.

Nevertheless, the specificity of Cuban society, formed by its multi-ethnic history, its revolutionary wars in the nineteenth century, and its more recent revolution, have produced particular forms of this religious reawakening. Afro-Cuban cults have emerged from clandestinity and are carried on openly in many areas, especially among the poorer people. The cult of saints traditional in Cuban society has taken on a fresh vigour, often mixed with practices stemming from the local people themselves. Certain devotions are really very popular in character, while others correspond more to the aspiration or expressions of a social middle class, the product of the social transformation of the revolution.

The churches are also seeing their attraction growing; this may be relative in extent, but in some cases it responds to the need to give a meaning to life in the midst of generalized disorientation. At the same time, the churches are rebuilding themselves institutionally, renewing their ethical and religious discourse, redefining their relations with other churches, and re-elaborating their relationship to the political authority. Many examples of such phenomena at work in Cuban society can be adduced: the issue of *Social Compass* (1994) devoted to socio-religious researches in Cuba provided a wealth of reflection to establish historical and contemporary bases for most of these. And yet the new situation has come about so rapidly that there are still no systematic researches that would allow us to establish general interpretations.

Among new religious phenomena I have mentioned the re-emergence of Santeria but this is not the only one. In a film such as *Fresa y Chocolate* (Strawberry and Chocolate), the religious dimension is very much to the fore, with its psychological manifestations, its functions of protection or help in obtaining material and cultural benefits, and also its aspect of auto-generation of new significances given to the images proceeding from the changing ecclesiastical institution.

On the other hand, the last declaration of the Cuban Catholic Bishops' Conference (1994, published on 16 May 1995) poses a very fundamental problem: the social and cultural unrest and the need to find a new meaning – which the Catholic institution thinks it can provide.

The Pentecostal churches are also flourishing. Their attraction is different from that of the historical churches, and they seem to respond to cultural and religious needs in various sectors of the population, among the poorer classes in towns and the country, but also among the new class that has emerged in the cities as a result of the revolution's successes in the fields of education, culture and work.

While the religions have never disappeared in Cuba during the revolutionary period, despite sometimes difficult relations between the political and the religious institutions, what has been happening in the last few years seems to be specific and linked to the changes affecting the whole of society in Cuba.

2. *Subjectivity and the market*

The revolutionary project in Cuba has tried to build a homogenous social and economic system, in which politics have guided the economy toward a more equitable distribution of material and cultural goods throughout the population. Despite numerous dfficulties, this social and cultural project has fulfilled many of its promises. Nevertheless, with the fall of the Soviet Union and the continued US blockade, the material bases of the socialist system have recently experienced a process of rapid and deep erosion. This is not the place to try to analyse the causes and mechanics of this in detail.

What it means, however, is that the political system is no longer in a position to carry out all its promises, and in many areas can do no more than provide the bare necessities for life – which is an achievement in itself, compared with the situation in other parts of the world that find themselves in a similar position. Faced with the impossibility of satisfying growing demands for both material and cultural consumer goods, it has been necessary to introduce not only major restrictions, but also elements of a market economy, thereby making some socialist economic norms – some of them too rigid in the past – more flexible.

If one reflects today on the capitalist market economy that dominates the global economy, one sees that its fundamental logic is the creation of an added value that can be translated into individual, or at least private, profit, leading to the accumulation of capital and allowing it to multiply. The creation of inequalities is thus a basis of economic activity and consequently of the whole of social and political life. In the capitalist system, it is the economy that effectively dominates the whole organization of society and imposes its values as parameters of the whole working of society. The socialist project, on the other hand, consists precisely in radically changing this type of situation, re-situating the economic system within the whole of societal activities. It is the political system that is responsible for establishing the norms of how society works, so as to assure – more or less successfully – a certain equality among human beings as social agents.

When a market economy is introduced, even with attempts at controls, this produces social and cultural effects that are very difficult to avoid. One of these is social and economic inequality. Inequalities can be socially acceptable if they are legitimized. This is done in different ways in different types of society: in pre-capitalist tributary societies, the relative inequality between different poles of society (local bodies and the State) was legitimzed by the importance of the service rendered, whether material or symbolic. In other forms of society, such as industrial capitalism, which produces great migrations of workers, especially from one continent to another, acceptance of inequalities between the classes was justified by the transitional character it had in the perception of the migrants. These all thought that their children could achieve a better situation in a society that valued social mobility, at least on the individual level. This was the case in the United States.

Other societies needed recourse to a meta-social legitimizing authority. This was particularly the case in mediaeval European societies. Recourse to divine authority was necessary to deal with the non-reciprocity of the landlord-tenant relationship. In present-day capitalism, legitimation of inequalities is a means of naturalizing social relationships, so that market forces come to be seen as fundamental laws of human nature. The market is the universal regulator, through its hidden hand. The possession of material goods and the possibility of accumulation are the result of work: the best win – i.e., those who have the greatest ability in economic or financial affairs.

In trying to ensure a basic equality through social measures and control of the economy, socialism guaranted a fairly universal, if somewhat uniform, security. With the introduction of the market, the political authority loses part of its capacity to organize the economy and is forced, rightly or otherwise, to liberalize some sectors of economic activity. This immediately leads to the establishment of new social relationships, which can be controlled up to a point, but which are needed to resolve immediate economic problems and to avoid the brutal dismantling of a social structure that was – in truth – too rigid in various aspects. In this process the political authority (party and state) loses part of its mobilizing capacity for creating a different society, and also, at least in some cases, its moral authority through the corruption that creeps in in some spheres. Zones of economic insecurity are established, along with a quest for a new balance. We know that when individuals or societies cannot resolve problems on the material level they try to find a solution in the symbolic field. This is a cultural constant, though it takes very different forms according to times and places. It is precisely here that religion has a role to play, as part of this symbolic universe with reference to a supernatural entity.

In Cuba, the new aspirations to consumption are proving very difficult to satisfy, especially during what is known as the 'special' period. At the same time, differences are growing and some individuals are being more fortunate in fulfilling their aspirations than others. A strong individualism is developing, ambivalent from an ethical standpoint, since on the one hand it favours major initiatives for the survival of the people but on the other it produces daily struggles at individual and family level and concentrates the greater part of people's aspirations on personal well-being and the activities that can contribute to this. The introduction of the market, even if not in its complete capitalist form, introduces this sort of contradiction into society. These are an inevitable outcome, even though they can to an extent be controlled. When political agents cannot reduce these contradictions on the macro-level of society as a whole, social agents try to reduce them on the micro-level, through their personal initiative, which opens up new areas for individualism.

Clearly, I am not saying that the socialist system that existed in Cuba until our day was devoid of contradictions. All I am trying to convey is the fact that new contradictions emerge with the introduction of the market. They can either be added to existing contradictions or eventually replace them. The need for individual and collective social agents to resolve them has always existed. In the present case, the new forms are of a more individual type. This is where the role of religion comes in.

Equally clearly, I am not reducing religion to this aspect – a point to which I shall come back. Religion cannot be identified with only some of its functions, even if these are authentic ones. What I am trying to show here is the coincidence that exists between the revitalization of religion taking place in Cuban society and the latter's transformation with the introduction of certain free-market elements. I am not going to say that the market is a factor in the religious revival, which would be falling into an extreme and ridiculous determinism. My purpose is to analyse these phenomena and discover the logics that might possibly exist in the relationships between them.

II. The ambivalence of religion

As I have already said, the social role played by religion can be ambivalent. Several aspects of this can be seen in the present situation in Cuba.

On the one hand, there is a close link between the development of individualism as a recognized and legitimate fact in the economic sphere and the development of certain Christian practices. In a competitive society economic resources are more uncertain and confront individuals with new situations they cannot foresee. In a socialist society, and particularly a poor one, in which the security of existence is well established but the possibilities of fulfilling more individual aspirations are limited, a certain philosophy of life develops, prizing the underlying well-being – even if this is minimal for all (the value of solidarity) – while on the other hand minimizing individual aspirations. When market elements are introduced, not only is the material basis changed, but social relationships are as well. Competitiveness between individuals increases, with a corresponding growth in the possibility of not achieving desired ends.

It is clear that in situations of shortage and great material difficulties, the introduction of this type of relationship has its effects in the religious sphere. Individuals seek help and protection in order to have all the intermediaries on their side and at the same time seek alleviation of their distress when these fail. Furthermore, the new, relatively antagonistic social relationships also unfold processes not only of self-protection but also of self-legitimation. Certain social groups need to be recognized as respectable, within new relationships generated by the market. Marks of respectability are sought, and religion can sometimes provide a basis for these. This is what happened in Western Europe when after the French Revolution part of the bourgeoisie returned to religion and its services as the expression – not necessarily a conscious one – of their excellence as a class.

In fact one can see a certain regression to elementary forms of religious beliefs and practices, self-generated, on the one hand as an adaptation to the new culture and on the other little influenced by what Antonio Gramsci called organic intellectuals in the field of religion. In Catholicism especially, there is a lack of specific religious agents to channel these manifestations. The success of new religious movements, especially of a Pentecostal nature, and the renaissance of Afro-Cuban religions, above all the Order of the *Orishas* (Yoruba spirits), are a response to this type of need.

The new economic relationships also impose a need to establish new ethical norms. The market system itself demands an internal ethic, without which it cannot function – respect for a deal. But the new situation poses much more basic ethical problems affecting the workings of the whole of society – the value of solidarity in the face of the possibility of private profit, the importance of the common good in the face of individual aspirations. In this sense a reference to religion can be a real service to society. This would mean a religious ethic based on gospel values, since Christians make up the majority of the religious population of Cuba, which would allow reference both to the utopia of the kingdom of God and to specific modes of action in social life.

I have spoken of the churches as institutions: one of their aspects is their relation to global society. Religious institutions define themselves as having a moral role not only in individual behaviour, but also in collective actions and in particular the exercise of political authority. The declaration of the Catholic bishops responds to this concern. This is a somewhat delicate matter, since we know that in the past the Catholic Church as an institution used the political regime in Cuba to ensure its existence and furtherance as an institution. After the revolution the position of the Catholic Church in Cuban society was clearly rather different. It had been the obligatory channel for any social recognition, especially among the poorer classes. In a society in which these classes carried no social and cultural weight but were, on the contrary, exploited and despised, the only way of being a person was to be baptized, perhaps married in church, and above all buried with religious ceremonies. Religious symbolism was the channel of social identity.

With the revolution, the popular classes gained social recognition, even if their material situation did not change from one day to the next. This immediately had the effect of toppling this social function of the Catholic Church and produced a sharp drop in the number of Catholic baptisms, weddings and funerals. The Catholic Church found itself in a minority in the new society of Cuba and had great difficulty in accepting this situation and adapting its behaviour accordingly. The climate of hostility engendered by the fact of the revolution and the subsequent actions of both party and church have not always – to put it mildly – helped to find the necessary balance.

With the opening of society to market elements, regarded as an opening to freedom – since in the general view of the Western world, market and freedom, like democracy and human rights, are linked together – the religious institutions have seen the possibility of developing new or renewed functions. On the one hand, they are making a real Christian ethical contribution, obviously limited to their sphere of real influence; on the other, however, concern for the institution can also provoke a desire to recover a lost role in Cuban society – which obviously produces great concern in political circles.

To end these remarks on the ambivalent nature of religion in a situation of economic, social, and cultural change, let me record one important fact. The role of religion cannot be interpreted in too mechanistic a fashion. Nor can the phenomenon of religion with its attendant social functions, however effective they may be, be completely identified. Remember that the religious world view includes a search for an overall meaning to human existence. This dimension transcends, in the sociological sense, all historical situations and forms of society. This is a verifiable fact: there is no strict linear evolution from a believing world to an atheist world, corresponding to a progress in human thought. This way of interpreting the history of thought belongs to a false modernity, against which various authors, particularly in the field of sociology of religion, are rightly reacting. Clearly, specific expressions of this search for meaning take forms that correspond to the culture and social structure of each society or group or social class (Houtart, 1992, 2). I am not seeking here to make a distinction between form and essence, but to say that within all these forms of religious expression we can find a search for an overall meaning with different ways of expressing this. Atheism is also a way of expressing overall meaning, which means that religions have no monopoly in this field.

The ambivalent character of religion has been well expressed in the film already mentioned, *Fresa y chocolate*. Clearly, social and cultural unrest provoke new religious expressions. The whole problem is to know which. Are we dealing with the sigh of the oppressed creature or a lever for a new leap forward? The answer cannot be dogmatic or *a priori*. We need to analyse the facts and try to interpret them from a sociological standpoint. This is what I turn to in the last part of this article: the theory and methodology of research.

III. Theory and methodology of research: critique of the post-modern critique of Marxist theory

1. The Marxist theory of religion

In an article on Karl Marx and Friedrich Engels as sociologists of religion, Michael Löwy has provided an excellent overview of the evolution of these founders of Marxism in regard to their analysis of religion. For Karl Marx, it is a producer of an ideal conditioned by material production and social relationships (Löwy, 1995, 41–5). He insisted on the conditioned nature of religious expressions. Engels added that religion is a symbolic space, staked out by antagonistic social forces. It is true that Engels sometimes gives a rather reductionist interpretation of the phenomenon of religion, as a cover-up, a mask for another reality made up of interest, needs and class rivalries, despite his excellent analyses of early Christianity, the Reformation, and the case of Thomas Münzer.

Dealing with the linkage between religion and the market, Engels analysed Calvinism in particular, considering that 'predestination was the religious expression of the fact that even in the commercial world of competition, success and failure did not depend on either human activity or capacity, but on circumstances beyond human control' (Engels, 1892, cited by Löwy, 1995, 47). This type of reflection is interesting because, in Engels' thought, the 'circumstances beyond human control' were higher and unknown economic forces. Today we are experiencing a strong reaction against such interpretations, and it is worth examining why.

2. The postmodern critique

Postmodernism is much discussed today. Its critique is made from philosophical, sociological, psychological and linguistic angles; the concept is also applied to art, music and architecture. It is not always easy to see exactly what is meant. I am going to approach the concept from the standpoint of sociology, and the sociology of religion in particular.

(a) Postmodernism as critique of the 'Age of Enlightenment'. The basic focus of the Enlightenment was that science was synonymous with truth and opposed to religion as interpretation of reality (Seidman, 1994). This philosophical orientation was adopted as the basis of all disciplines of human knowledge. There was an identification of knowledge with truth and a degree of imposition of a scientistic rationalism as the universal parameter. This thought was taken furthest in the 'exact sciences', but also applied to history and the social sciences. Scientific understanding was like a revelation, liberating humankind from its alienations. Each sector of human knowledge was elevated into a particular science with its own norms and methods.

The postmodern critique is first a critique of the suppositions of the Enlightenment. It seeks to move beyond its philosophical approach without denying its contributions, in order to re-structure understanding within society. Part of the postmodern approach seeks to study and understand the social conditions for the emergence of understanding. In this sense, it questions the scientific certitudes of the past and quests for new, less compartmentalized ways of reasoning.

Since there was, in Western societies, an intimate connection between knowledge and power, postmodernity also takes a critical stance with regard to this result of the Age of Enlightenment. Among its principal exponents, Michael Foucault (Foucault, 1977) and Jean François Lyotard (Lyotard, 1984) affirm that the postmodern reaction is linked to the rebellious spirit of the 1960s and 1970s, especially in France. There was a generalized critique of modernity, directed according to media and exponents either at capitalism for its social, cultural, class, gender and sex exclusions or at Marxism for the totalitarian tendencies of socialist states and the lack of space they allowed to subjectivity. This reaction also stressed individual values and experience as a basis for interpreting reality.

(b) Science is not neutral. One postmodernist statement is the need to demystify science as pure objectivity. In fact no science is purely objective, since it is conditioned not only by the type of culture in which it functions, but also by its social and economic environment. What is valid for science as a whole is, says Steven Seidman, even more true of social theories, which reveal the point of view of those who enunciate them. He gives the example of feminist writers who state that 'understanding is always produced from a specific social position, giving voice to particular values, interests and beliefs' (Seidman, 1994, 10).

Postmodernism also criticizes Max Weber's claim that scientific work is neutral and objective, especially as regards the social sciences. Clearly, this discovery that science is not neutral is not really a new contribution. When one reads what Marx and Engels wrote on the subject of power and knowledge, one can find this sort of critique already in place. Many others have also made a contribution and there was no need to wait for postmodernism to criticize Max Weber.

(c) Abandonment of universal categories and grand explanatory theories. An absolutely basic tenet of this new school is the coercive nature of any global thinking that pretends to devise universal categories valid throughout time and space. At the same time it attacks explanatory theories that seek to provide a reason for the totality of human phenomena. For postmodernism, the multiplicity of subjects and understandings reflects their varying localizations within history. What matters is to escape from systems offering a single key, to return to discover particularities. In this sense there is a radical critique of what postmodernists call fundamentalism, in the sense of a thought-system or body of knowledge that founds the totality of a discipline. Finally, postmodernism criticizes the theory of enlightenment itself: this type of general knowledge, it claims, which considers itself a step towards human liberty and finally liberation, in fact promotes ethnocentric interests under a mask of universality. In this sense it also attacks Marxism for its claims to be scientific and to have discovered the true laws governing history and society. Postmodernism defines itself as post-structuralism and post-Marxism, very much under the influence of the events of May 1968 in France.

(d) The social sciences as interpretation and mediation, not explanation. Postmodernism particularly attacks the social sciences for claiming to provide an explanation of the collective human situation. Such an

explanation, it argues, is impossible, because what is human is particular, but also because it implies the imposition of a cultural and ultimately social and political power, which prevents true discovery of the social agent in his/her particularity.

Thierry Verhelst provides a good description of this approach:

> It is a question of a counter-method. This has to be sought in the area of hermeneutics: interpretation of texts, and beyond these, of all forms of human expression. The explanatory method of the natural sciences is opposed by the comprehensive method of the human sciences, 'capable of seizing the meaning of lived experience in its particularity'. Popper, Kuhn, and Feyerabend have demonstrated the interpretative character of the 'exact' sciences: these were never simple descriptions of reality 'such as it is', for the reason that human understanding springs from a personal creative act (Verhelst, 1995, 15).

Steven Seidman states that sociology has undergone a process of progressive insularity of its theory, because of its explanatory claims. An empirical approach does not resolve the explanatory conflicts. For example, these come to the fore when we try to interpret the type of discriminations current in societies today – class or race or gender? The same holds for defining Western societies: are they post-industrial or late-capitalist? Other examples could be adduced, but, says Seidman, there is no future for an explanatory sociology trying to provide acceptable lines in general fashion. A consensus is possible on certain points, such as the relationship between the social agent and structure, or between micro- and macro-dimensions, or the interconnection between social structure and culture. Nonetheless, he claims, we have to move from a sociological theory as founding practice to narrative understandings that unite social analysis with a moral standpoint. The dominant point of view of the Enlightenment was precisely its affirmation that there exists a general ahistorical and neutral knowing subject.

(e) The parcelization of understanding. Such a position leads inevitably to the parcelization and even individualization of understanding. If there are no universal categories but only particular ones, and if explanatory theories are interpreted as impositions from a particular standpoint, the only solution is to find reality in particular human experience. Hence the idea of hermeneutics and the reading of social realities in the form of texts, as symbolic expressions. Against what postmodernism calls a culture of intellectual, scientific and political control, it proposes the rediscovery of the individual as the source of understanding.

Zygmund Bauman has adopted a very radical stance in this respect. For him, postmodernism signifies the collapse of the boundaries between disciplines and the loss of a social or epistemological centre. The social world is fragmented into a multiplicity of communities, cultural traditions and understandings. He proposes that social analysis should abandon any pretension to explain social phenomena in order to become a mediator among the different social worlds, as an interpreter of cultural cross-currents and an advocate of particular moral visions.

Seidman also defines postmodern social analysis as a hermeneutical investigation, similar to literary criticism, examining communities as 'texts' with a view to translating the unfamiliar into the familiar, legitimizing differences, increasing tolerance, encouraging diversity, and collaborating in establishing understanding and communication among different groups (Siedman, 1984, 14–15).

This postmodernist approach obviously has repercussions on the analysis of religious phenomena. There is nothing more symbolic, in its view, than the sphere of religion, and so this is more impossible than any other sphere to systematize in an overall manner or to express in universal categories. In this sense, postmodernism appeals to Mircea Eliade. There is thus a postmodern view of the study of religions; this is closer to a phenomenology of religion than to a sociology in the strict sense of the word as expounded by Durkheim, Marx or Weber.

(f) Critique of the postmodernist position. What can be said about the postmodernist critique is that it tends not to apply a part of its focus to its own position. We are entitled to ask: why does it reject totality, explanation, theory, and why is there this explosion of subjectivity, of the role of the individual? Without descending to over-mechanistic interpretations, we can note a coincidence between the postmodern wave and the progressive weakening of the three great pillars of social cohesion since the Second World War. These are: the model elaborated for Western societies by Keynes and Ford; what Samir Amin called the Bandung era, meaning the nationalist and populist regimes of the Third World; and finally the socialist model in the countries of Eastern Europe (Samir Amin, 1994).

The causes of this weakening and final collapse, at least in some cases, can be linked to a multiplicity of factors. In the Western world, which produced postmodernism, there has been an eruption of new social conflicts since the 'Golden Sixties', with a declining level of consumption spreading through the lower social orders and into the middle classes, coupled with the beginnings of a neo-liberal wave designed to strengthen the multiplication of capital. The upheavals of May 1968 were an explicit reaction against the capitalist economic model and the type of rationality it had developed, which was invading the whole domain of values and to a degree destroying subjectivity. Neo-liberalism increased the stress on individuals, their interests, their potential for competition, and their aspirations. The collapse of the socialist regimes in Europe provided postmodernism with confirmation of its thesis concerning the individual and subjectivity.

In this sense, as Alejandro Serrano, former rector of the National University of Nicaragua, said, postmodernism is the ideological wing of contemporary capitalism. In a sense, there is nothing more helpful than to parcel out reality, deny the existence of sweeping theories, combat the idea of systems, and exalt the individual, while at the same time the extension of capitalism is making it the only world-wide system and it is accentuating the class struggle on a global scale, but through new devices that most people find difficult to perceive.

The study of religion also reveals crises in its institutional bodies and a great growth of new religious movements, especially of a Pentecostalist type. This also corresponds to the same general orientation: analysis of these movements and crises, using the intellectual tools of postmodernism, points to the uniqueness of each situation and the development of subjectivity, while it keeps quiet about the link between religious phenomena and the various consequences of the global spread of the capitalist system.

3. A Marxist appraisal of the new religious situation

I am not going to develop this approach at length, as this has already been done by various authors, both before the birth of postmodernism and in the present situation. One thinks of Georg Lukacs, who despite his self-criticism made a real contribution to the critique of knowledge (Lukacs, 1960); also of Antonio Gramsci, who noted the specificity of the religious phenomenon and analysed it as a part of the overall social phenomenon (Portelli, 1974). Closer to the present, there is Maurice Godelier, who insisted on 'the ideal part of the real', that is, the importance of thought in the construction of social relationships. Religion obviously has its role as one of the forms taken by the ideal (Godelier, 1986). In his introductory article to the issue of *Social Compass* devoted to Cuba, Jorge Ramirez Calzadilla tackles the same subject in relation to defining religion and the religious understanding (*Social Compass*, 1994, 1988). In a recent work I, too, have tried to explain what a Marxist appraisal means for the study of religious phenomena, without falling into philosophical determinism (Houtart, 1992).

The most recent essay on this subject is the article by Michael Löwy on Marx and Engels as sociologists of religion (Löwy, 1995). He claims that a Marxist appraisal must first take the totality of the phenomenon into account, which contradicts the postmodernist tendency that accuses this way of thinking of imposing a straitjacket on its approach to reality and claims that the fact of studying reality through consideration of its totality implies a heuristic function where the social sciences are concerned. It means that a complex of questions is raised on the subject of each study, even if this is of a particular phenomenon, without thereby destroying the object itself. Clearly – and here postmodernism is right – questioning of reality as a whole is not done except from a point of view that might be called pre-sociological. In their analysis of religion, Marx and Engels started from the situation of the 'submerged' classes and studied religion from this concern – for a typical example of Marx's methodology in this respect, see his study of Louis Bonaparte and the 18 Brumaire (Marx, 1976).

In a way we also need to make a critique of the Marxist appraisal, since it has in fact led to somewhat erroneous interpretations and explanations of religious phenomena, at times showing no understanding of the object of its inquiry. There are some aspects of Marx's thought, especially in its philosophical phase, that cannot be used in contemporary investigations. In particular, we have to abandon all that is redolent of scientistic discourse, typical of its (modern) time; we also have to avoid reproducing a certain concept of historical determinism that takes the revolutionary process as its only subject. On the other hand, his dialectical perspective allows us to interpret religion with great flexibility, without losing the connections with other social factors and without losing sight of the many mediations in these connections.

In appraising the religious situation in Cuba today, a Marxist approach would first have to take account of the combined economic, social, political, and cultural evolution of the country. On the basis of this, it would study all the necesary details, as the Department of Socio-religious Studies has done, of the new forms, expressions and orientations of the various religions. There is a delicate but necessary process of reflection to establish hypotheses for understanding the relationships that can exist between the new religious phenomena and the introduction of elements of a market economy in Cuba, without falling into either reductionism or any sort of idealism.

Translated by Paul Burns

Bibliography

1960 Lukacs, G., *Histoire et conscience de classe*. Paris
1974 Portelli, H., *Gramsci et la question religieuse*, Paris
1975 'Marxism and Sociology of Religion', *Social Compass*, Vol. XXII/3–4
1976 Marx, K., *Le 18 Brumaire de Louis Bonaparte*, Paris

1977 Foucault, M., *Power/Knowledge*, New York
1986 Godelier, M., *Lo ideal y lo material*, Madrid
1988 'New Marxist Readings on Religion', *Social Compass*, Vol.XXXV/2–3
1992 Houtart, F., *Ruptures sociales et religion*, Paris
——, *Sociología de la religión*, Havana
1994 Amin, S. 'La nouvelle mondialisation capitaliste', *Alternatives Sud*, Vol. 1, no. 1, 19–44
Argüelles Mederos, 'Les systèmes divinatoires de la règle Ocha', *Social Compass*, Vol. 41, no. 2, 293–301
Bienefeld, M., 'The Case against Market Socialism', *New Politics*, Spring, 157–63
Lyotard, J. F., *The Postmodern Condition*, Minneapolis
Ramirez Calzadilla, J., 'Les recherches socio-religieuses à Cuba', *Social Compass*, Vol. 41, no. 2, 195–202
Seidman, S., *The Postmodern Turn – New Perspectives on Social Theories*, Cambridge
1995 'Declaración del Consejo Permanente de la Conferencia de los Obispos Católicos de Cuba', 16 May
Löwy, M., 'Karl Marx et Friedrich Engels comme sociologues de la religion', *Archives des sciences sociales des religions*, No. 89, Jan-Mar, 41–52
Ortega, J., 'Identidad y postmodernidad en América Latina', *Socialismo y participación*, no. 70, July, 41–52
Verhelst, T, 'Sens et société: la sociologie en question et un défi pour le réseau culture', *Cultures et développement*, No. 22/6, 14–16

Oriental Religions and the Market

Bernard Teo

Asia is geographical shorthand for a huge continent comprising a very diverse range of ancient and more recent civilizations, historically hostile nations, ethnic groups and cultures. Its countries stretch from the Indian sub-continent to the Pacific rim and South-east Asia. Just as disparate are its religious faiths. There are millions of professed adherents to Hinduism, Buddhism, Islam, Shintoism, Christianity, Taoism, Confucianism and other forms of religious animism.

Given this reality, it would be impossible for me to cover satisfactorily the whole area indicated in the title above. So I will limit my article to a reflection on the debates that are currently taking place in the Asia/Pacific regions on the impact of the market on some Asian cultures, particularly those influenced by Confucianism, since it is the predominant ethos of a large part of Asia. Being a citizen from Singapore, I thought the Singapore experience would be a good place to reflect on the issues. Not only is it a thriving cosmopolitan city with a multi-racial, multi-cultural and multi-religious populace, it is also a place where one experiences both the convergences and divergences of the East and West.

The emergent East

In the second half of this century, a strong commitment to the free-market economy and openness to Western industrial technology have led many countries in the Asian and Pacific rim to experience an unprecedented growth in wealth and economic power for the first time in the history of the region. Japan has risen from the ashes of her comprehensive defeat in World War II to become an economic super-power. China, a latecomer in the game, is expected to become the next economic super-power by the third decade of the next millennium. Taiwan, Hong Kong, Singapore and South Korea are known as the 'Tiger' or the new industrial economies. Other emerging economies include the south-east Asian countries of

Malaysia, Indonesia, Brunei and Thailand, with probably Vietnam, Burma and the Philippines in tow.

In the light of these developments, there is a deep conviction within academic and political circles in the Asian region that the Asian continent is at an important and exciting crossroad of human history. People believe that by the next century, the balance of economic power will gradually shift from the industrialized societies of the West to the East.

East versus West

These developments stimulate much discussion in Asia about the impact of industrialization and affluence on many Asian societies and cultures. A current trend in economic, social and political discourse is the debate on the importance of differences in culture and values between East and West. Among many academics and politicians, it is fashionable to attribute the boom in the region primarily to Asian culture and values, particularly those espoused by Confucianism (Confucian-based cultures include China, Japan, Korea, Taiwan, Hong Kong, Vietnam and Singapore). What is becoming clear in these discourses is that Western culture and values are subject to growing criticism and rejection.

When international tensions arise in trade and justice issues, their root causes lie in perceived differences in value priorities affecting the way of doing things between East and West. For example, Japan in its trade disputes with the US defended itself in terms of its uniqueness as a society with its own unique Asian way of doing things. Accusations of human-rights abuses in China, Burma, Singapore, Malaysia and Indonesia are often dismissed in terms of Asian ways of understanding human rights and social priorities in contrast to the Western understanding of human rights and priorities. The Malaysian Prime Minister, Dr Mahathir, sees Western culture and values as decaying and so resents very much the imposition of Western ways of thinking about human rights and development on his country. Mr Lee Kuan Yew, Singapore's former Prime Minister and a major proponent of a return to Asian values and roots, perhaps best encapsulates the attitude of most Asian leaders towards Western culture and values. When he was asked what was wrong with the American system, he said: 'It is not my business to tell people what's wrong with their system. It is my business to tell people not to foist their system indiscriminately on societies in which it will not work.'[1] This answer implies that not all Western concepts of democracy and human rights are applicable to Asian societies.

Eastern culture as a bulwark against the West

It seems ironic that at a point of history when many Asian societies are experiencing an emerging confidence in themselves and in their place in the world, there is a growth in hostility towards the West and its values. How does one explain this, when Western models of progress and development were what the East were trying to emulate and achieve? Why is there this surge in interest and pride in Eastern cultures and values? After all, many of Asia's leaders and elite were trained and educated in the West. It would be naive to think that they would be totally unaffected by their exposure to Western cultures, practices, and mores; or that there is nothing about the West that is admired and worthy of aspiration. Otherwise, how does one explain the fact that many offspring of Asia's elite, togther with the best and brightest of its youth, are still being sent to the best universities of the West? Furthermore, many of Asia's political and judicial systems are influenced to a great extent by Western models because of the colonial legacy.

I would suggest two reasons for this reaction. Firstly, some Asian states have varying degrees of authoritarian regimes, both benevolent and malevolent. Emphases on human rights and justice issues that the West considers to be priorities, especially those that concern the individual, would upset the political order and the authority of the powers that be. There is this fear that political practices which might work for Western societies would only create chaos for Eastern societies if they were indiscriminately applied.

Secondly, and more importantly, many of Asia's elite do not like certain directions that some contemporary Western industrial societies are taking. What they see is the gradual breakdown of Western civil society in the proliferation of violence and firearms, in the ease of access to drugs, and in the loss of shame and civic behaviour. There is a belief that the primary ethos responsible for this state of affairs is the over-emphasis on democracy and the dogma of the inviolability of individual rights. These are upheld at the expense of an orderly society. Furthermore, there is a belief that the decay of civil society is accelerated by the breakdown of the family as the basic building block of society.

In this context, the current Asian interest in cultural differences between East and West is really a search for an alternative ethos within the rich cultural and religious traditions of the East that could provide a coherent defence against those Western influences that contribute to the erosion of social cohesion and to the breakdown of civic society. Furthermore, the return to the roots of Eastern cultural and religious values is part of the search for a new and Asian identity. They would serve as bulwarks against the perceived arrogant imposition of the virtues of Western democratic ideals on the rest of the world.

Consequently, some of the radical questions facing the newly prosperous industrial societies of Asia are these. How can we enjoy the wealth and prosperity generated by an industrial economy without our societies going the way of Western industrial societies? Given that human history is littered with the experiences of the rise and fall of many cultures and civilizations in both the East and the West, must decline be inevitable? Why do cultures decline in the first place? Is it possible to stave off this decline? Are there values within our rich Confucian-based cultural and religious traditions that could help us to continue to build on our rise at this point of history, while retaining a cherished sense of community and social cohesion?

The quest for answers to these questions has led particularly those societies that are Confucian-based (China, Korea, Japan, Vietnam, Hong Kong and Singapore) to a coherent and systematic identification of values which make them tick. A Confucian-based society values social harmony. Hence a well-ordered society is paramount for the maximum enjoyment of human freedom. It believes that restraints on individual rights and liberty are necessary for social harmony and functioning. The good of the community is primary, while the good of the individual is secondary.

Eastern societies hold the strong belief that the individual is not a self-enclosed monad but exists in the context of the family. The family in turn is the basic building block of society. It unfolds into the extended family, and into friends, and then ends in the wider network of society. The value of self-reliance, aided by one's extended family and social-support group, explains the strong aversion of many Asian societies to state welfarism. The ruler or the government does not try to provide what the lower units of society could provide on their own level.

Confucian-based cultures treasure the values of thrift, hard work, filial piety, loyalty in the extended family, and, above all, respect for authority, scholarship and learning. There is also a tradition of strict discipline and respect for the teacher.

It is hoped that the identification and inculcation of these 'Asian' values to the young and future generations will ensure the continued survival and economic growth of Asian societies for generations to come.

The debates on culture – which way to go?

In these debates, one may ask whether the moral breakdown in Western cultures is not attributable to the inherent shortcomings in Western culture or values as such. I suspect not. Rather, I suspect that Western decline is not attributable to those values as such, but to the destructive bias inherent in a successful and affluent society, whether before the Industrial Revolution or after it. A precious lesson to be learnt from the history of successful societies is that as wealth and power accumulates, corruption and decline seems to be an inevitable consequence.

For the past four hundred years, continual economic and industrial growth and technological change have certainly transformed the Western culture and experience. However, the major drawback is that society gradually implodes towards self-centred individualism.

A similar phenomenon is now spreading through Asia's new industrial economies. Under the impact of economic growth, technological change and social transformation over the past five decades, the cultures and experience of the East have changed. The family-centred Confucian-based Asian societies are definitely moving rapidly toward self-centred individualism. The relentless pursuit of material success becomes the measure of one's worth and standing in society. Hence Eastern families are also caught in the same social problems of change. We have more broken families, the abandonment of the sick elderly, and a breakdown in school discipline and respect for authority in the schools. Parents spend a lot less time with each other and with their children as they pursue material rewards and success in the market place. As women are more educated and become more independent financially, they have higher expectations and no longer believe they have to put up with unhappy marriages. In Singapore, this new status of women has led many of them to experience difficulty in finding a life-partner in a marriage commitment, partly because the traditional role of the male as the provider is no longer clear. In this light, Mr Lee himself expressed regret that he had ever educated the women of Singpore!

A local Singaporean academic wrote a strong negative critique of the younger generation of Singaporeans growing up in a relatively peaceful and affluent environment that is rapidly modernizing and very open to the cultural influences of the West:

Increasingly, acquisitiveness has become the very soul of society, penetrating almost every aspect of social life and thought. Everything has a price attached to it, so much so that Singaporeans, especially during the 1970s when the economy grew by leaps and bounds, appeared to be fast developing a system of values according to which the worth or significance of any person, object, or activity was calculated exclusively in terms of his or its potential or actual pecuniary value. It was the market value (an expression which was used with increasing frequency) of any person, his services or his goods in terms of dollars and cents which mattered most; and anything which was not reducible to such quantitative terms (for example love, courage, honour, sacrifice, integrity, selflessness, each with its irreducible qualitative wholeness) was largely ignored or at best regarded with mild contempt.[2]

His observations are on target. What is clear is that a successful market economy has also brought about a social transformation that is worrying to the Singapore authorities. Of course, Singapore is not the only case in the Asian region. China, for example, has been warning its citizens in recent times against greed and materialism. What is clear is that those characteristics that the elites of the East saw as undesirable in the West are rearing their ugly heads in the East.

While these negative trends are undeniably present in the new industrial economies, an interesting but positive trend is also noticeably emerging. The experience of wealth, prosperity and success has certainly not fulfilled the deepest aspirations of the human heart, but has led to a discernible search for a deeper meaning and purpose to life. In Singapore, the early Chinese were predominantly adherents of Taoism or Buddhism, or practised ancestor worship. The search for answers to the deeper questions of life has led many to shed the religious beliefs of their Chinese forebears in which they were brought up, and to replace them with more satisfactory alternatives. Some have professed agnosticism as a preference, while more and more Chinese today are converting to Christianity.

It is clear that there are shared characteristics in the human experiences of the affluent and industrialized societies common to all the East and West. While I can understand and appreciate the apprehensions of many of Asia's leaders that their societies may possibly decline the way of the West, I am not at all convinced that the current debates in the East on culture and the search for alternatives should draw such a sharp contrast between Eastern and Western values or emphasize the superiority of one over the other. If one is not careful, the return to Eastern values, because of its emphasis on the priority of the community over the individual, could be used to reinforce malevolent authoritarian regimes in the name of social order.

I am not convinced that the differences between Eastern and Western values are irreconcilable. This is because many of the esteemed values in Asian societies such as thrift, hard work, the importance of love for one's family, respect for authority, the good of the community, respect for scholarship and learning were also the very values cherished in, and very much a part of, Western culture. I do not think that they are very different from some aspects of classical Protestant work ethic.

We are indeed at an important crossroads of human history. Rather than retreat into our Eastern cultures and traditions against those of the West, I believe that the more viable alternative is to search for universal human values to underpin and humanize the dynamism of both Asian and Western industrial societies. That will be our contribution to a global consciousness of our shared humanity and destiny.

Bibliography

Jon S. T. Quah (ed.), *In Search of Singapore's National Values*, Singapore 1990
Kernial S. Sandhu and Paul Wheatley (ed.), *Management of Success: The Moulding of Singapore*, Singpore 1989
Julia Ching, *Chinese Religions*, Maryknoll 1993
——, *Confucianism and Christianity: A Comparative Study*, Tokyo 1977

Notes

1. Fared Zakaria, 'Culture is Destiny: A Conversation with Lee Kuan Yew', *Foreign Affairs* 73.2, 110.
2. Ho Wing Meng, 'Value Premises Underlying the Transformation of Singapore', in *Management of Success*, 678.

III · The Market and Ethics

The Market and Catholic Social Teaching

David Hollenbach

The institutions of the market place can have both positive and negative consequences for the dignity of human persons and the common good of society. Thus the Catholic Church's official ethical teaching neither simply endorses nor simply rejects the market. Rather, it seeks to encourage those dimensions of market economics with positive consequences and to criticize those with negative outcomes.

John Paul II's 1991 encyclical, *Centesimus Annus*, addressed the question of the significance of the collapse of Communism for the church's stand toward market capitalism. The pope asked whether this revolutionary change means that capitalism has been victorious and should be endorsed as that appropriate economic system for the newly independent countries of Eastern Europe, the developing countries of the Third World and indeed the whole global system. John Paul II's response to this question deserves quotation at some length:

> The answer is obviously complex. If by 'capitalism' is meant an economic system which recognizes the fundamental and positive role of business, the market, private property and the resulting responsibility for the means of production, as well as free human creativity in the economic sector, then the answer is certainly in the affirmative, even though it would perhaps be more appropriate to speak of a 'business economy', 'market economy' or simply 'free economy'. But if by 'capitalism' is meant a system in which freedom in the economic sector is not circumscribed within a strong juridical framework which places it at the service of human freedom in its totality, and which sees it as a particular aspect of that freedom, the core of which is ethical and religious, the answer is certainly negative.[1]

The hypothetical formulation suggests a distinction between the processes and institutions of the market on the one hand and the values these institutions promote or impede on the other. If and when markets promote human dignity, social solidarity and justice, they receive moral approbation. If and when markets impede the realization of these values, their operation should be restricted or limited. Thus markets are not good or bad in themselves. They are to be judged ethically in the light of their consequences.

Catholic social teaching thus judges markets in line with Augustine's distinction between the useful good (*bonum utile*) and goods that are intrinsically valuable. This distinction between instrumental values and those that are good or evil in themselves serves as a warning against one-dimensional ideologies. It implies that both free-market systems and alternatives to them have to be evaluated from a perspective that transcends the purview of instrumental economic rationality. In the passage cited above, John Paul II identifies this higher viewpoint as one that attends to 'human freedom in its totality'. Such a perspective on economic questions follows from the church's properly religious concerns. The church's religious mission puts it on guard against economic reductivism.

For example, all the modern social encyclicals firmly rejected the historical materialism and atheism of Leninist ideology. This ideology collapsed the full range of values that need to be considered in assessing economic life into those present in structures of economic power and production. Though analysis of these structures is very important in reaching ethical economic judgments, it is not sufficient. Indeed it becomes self-defeating when it is regarded as sufficient, for action based on such one-dimensional analysis undermines the creativity and initiative that are rooted in human freedom in its fullness. This opposition to economic reductionism served as a platform for sustained church resistance to Communist rule.

In a similar way, church teachings have warned against the individualism of *laissez-faire* market systems. Though free markets can be an expression of human freedom, they do not adequately reflect the full scope of what human beings require for their well-being and what they are capable of achieving together. An ideology that treats market freedom as a quasi-absolute gives individual autonomy a one-sided importance and effectively denies the social nature of human existence and the communal dimensions of freedom. Such reductivist individualism also neglects the fundamental requirements of Christian love of neighbour. As the Second Vatican Council put it, 'God's plan gives the human vocation a communitarian nature' and 'more that an individualistic ethic is required'.[2]

Equally important to this sort of critique of reductivist ideologies today, however, is the way church teaching has assessed economic ideas in light of their concrete outcomes and practical usefulness for the promotion of human well-being. In the post-Cold War era, the black-and-white struggle between ideologies that affirm the benefits of markets and those that deny them has largely come to an end. The issue now is what kind of market economy should be pursued in the future and how much of social life should be organized according to market principles. The various aspects and tendencies of markets, therefore, need to be assessed in light of their practical usefulness in advancing human well-being rather than simply defended or criticized in broad ideological terms.

Historically the Catholic tradition of ethical reflection has been considerably more pragmatic and open to learning from experience in addressing economic questions than in the areas of sexual ethics and some aspects of bioethics in recent years. The church's world-wide, transnational extent has given it vital experience of nearly all of the economic systems that have been developed, and its historical memory is a long one. Thus there is an experiential basis for the reluctance of church teaching to support any one economic programme as the best economic regime. Papal encyclicals from Leo XIII's *Rerum Novarum* in 1891 to John Paul II's *Centesimus Annus* in 1991 have often appealed to this experience in pointing out the negative consequences of both market capitalism and state socialism. The market, operating on its own terms alone, can have very destructive effects on working people, on the environment, and especially on the poor. The failure of the state socialism of the former Communist bloc has led some to celebrate the power of market capitalism uncritically. The presence of the church in societies experiencing the negative consequences of both systems has made its official teachings wary of endorsing one system because of the perceived limitations of the other. This experience and historical memory can make useful contributions in assessing the place and limits of markets today.

In practice Communist state socialism led not only to loss of political freedom but to loss of efficiency and productivity as well, as the economic difficulties of the former Soviet Union revealed. The critique of 'really existing socialism' in *Centesimus Annus* was based in part on the inefficiency of Communist economic programmes. In the view of the encyclical, this inefficiency was not simply a technical problem, but 'rather a consequence of the violation of human rights to private initiative, to ownership of property and to freedom in the economic sector'.[3] Lacking the space for this freedom and initiative, Communist societies stagnated because they lacked the creativity needed to serve the material well-being of their members more adequately.

John Paul, therefore, affirms the efficiency and productivity of market economies. And he endorses entrepreneurship and economic initiative in terms that remind one of Max Weber's discussion of the 'Protestant ethic'.[4] But the pope also repeatedly appeals to the history and experience of peoples living under capitalist, market-based systems to warn against moving from the inadequacy of state socialism to uncritical support for markets. In market-based societies, he observes, many persons are unable to participate in the market place because they lack the resources needed to do so. The following passage is illustrative: 'The fact is that many people, perhaps the majority today, do not have the means which would enable them to take their place in an effective and humanly dignified way within a productive system in which work is truly central . . . Thus, if not actually exploited, they are to a great extent marginalized; economic development takes place over their heads.'[5] The pope's argument is here in full agreement with the United States Catholic bishops statement that 'basic justice demands the establishment of minimum levels of participation in the life of the human community for all persons'.[6] The lack of such participation continues to be present in advanced societies 'in conditions of "ruthlessness" in no way inferior to the darkest moments of the first phase of industrialization'. It is the condition in which 'the great majority of people in the Third World still live'. And on the global level, 'the chief problem [for poor countries] is that of gaining fair access to the international market'.[7] The pope calls the conditions that lead to such marginalization 'structures of sin which impede the full realization of those who are in any way oppressed by them'.[8] And he says the church can contribute to an 'authentic theory and praxis of liberation' through its social teaching and its 'concrete commitment and material assistance in the struggle against marginalization and suffering'.[9]

Thus the collapse of Eastern European economic models should not be confused with the victory of what we might call 'really existing capitalism'. For example, *Centesimus Annus* says that 'it is unacceptable to say that the defeat of so-called "Real Socialism" leaves capitalism as the only model of economic organization'.[10] Or again, after discussing the continuing reality of marginalization and exploitation, especially in the Third World, and the reality of human alienation, especially in advanced societies, the pope adds a strong note of warning: 'The collapse of the Communist system in so many countries certainly removes an obstacle to facing these problems in an appropriate and realistic way, but it is not enough to bring about their solution. Indeed there is a risk that a radical capitalist ideology should spread which refuses even to consider these problems, in the *a priori* belief that any attempt to solve them is doomed to failure, and that blindly entrusts their solution to the free development of market forces.'[11]

Earlier church teachings had taken a similar stance. For example, Leo XIII was strongly aware of how unconstrained market institutions can lead to situations in which 'a small number of very rich men have been able to lay upon the masses of poor [*infinitae proletariorum multitudini*] a yoke little better than slavery itself'.[12] To prevent this, workers must be guaranteed a living wage, humane working conditions, the right to organize and strike, and governmental protection from exploitation.[13] These themes run through all the later social encyclicals and they call for definite limits on the operation of free markets. They are evident in *Centesimus Annus'* call for markets to be 'circumscribed within a strong juridical framework'. Such a framework of law is necessary to avoid 'making market mechanisms the only point of reference for social life'. For example, some social controls envisioned include 'a solid system of social security and professional training, the freedom to join trade unions and the effective action of unions, the assistance provided in cases of unemployment, the opportunities for democratic participation in the life of society'. Both society and state are called upon to protect workers 'from the nightmare of unemployment' by seeking 'balanced growth and full employment' and 'through unemployment insurance and retraining programmes'. Wages must be adequate for living in dignity, 'including a certain amount for savings'. And legislation is needed to block exploitation 'of those on the margins of society', including immigrants.[14]

Catholic social teaching founds this practical critique of both unimpeded markets and of stifling state control on an anthropology that can be called personalist communitarianism. It is personalist in its insistence that the dignity, worth and freedom of all human beings must be fully respected in the economic as well as the political domains. It is communitarian in stressing that this dignity and freedom can only be realized in solidarity and communal interdependence. This anthropology is reflected in the first three chapters of the Second Vatican Council's *Gaudium et Spes*, which were devoted to the dignity of the human person, the community of humankind, and the value of human activity and labour.[15] The significance of work, which is one of the central foci of the church's economic ethic, can only be grasped when human dignity is understood in solidaristic or communal terms. People do not work alone. They do not achieve greater freedom through ever-increasing solitude. They cannot attain economic well-being by simply being left alone, as some apologists for market freedom would have it. The anthropology of the Council and of the social encyclicals is thus diametrically opposed to that found in libertarian market theory. Milton Friedman, the Nobel Prize-winning economist whose libertarian thought has been widely influential, compares the agents in the marketplace to an isolated, self-sufficient, island-dwelling household (a small group of 'Robinson Crusoes') making rational decisions about whether to engage in trade with other such households on other islands.[16] Catholic social thought rejects this image as entirely inadequate. Persons are bound together in a web of interdependence that precedes the choices they make, the trade they engage in, and the contracts they agree to. Indeed Pope John XXIII observed that this interdependence is growing stronger due to the complexifying technology and enhanced communication of contemporary social life.[17]

This solidaristic anthropology has practical implications for the assessment of the proper scope of markets. Successful entrepreneurship, for example, is based on the knowledge of the needs of others and the development of creative ways of meeting those needs. *Centesimus Annus* argues that it 'requires the cooperation of many people working toward a common goal' for it to be a source of wealth in modern society. Further, the ability to engage in successful entrepreneurship depends on 'the possession of know-how, technology and skill' that can only be acquired in co-operation with others through education and the sharing of knowledge.[18] Thus entrepreneurial activity depends on 'ever more extensive working communities' bound together 'by a progressively expanding chain of solidarity'.[19]

These observations about the growing interdependence of economic life today have been the occasion of an interesting rethinking of private property in *Centesimus Annus*. The earlier social encyclicals drew upon biblical, patristic and scholastic sources when they maintained that the earth and its natural resources were created by God for the benefit of the whole human community, not for private individuals. Thomas Aquinas argued that private ownership is a practically efficient way of organizing the distribution of material things and that it encourages responsible stewardship for them. This practical justification of private ownership, however, is limited by the more basic purpose of material goods – meeting the needs of all. 'In cases of need, all things are common property, so that there would seem to be no sin in taking another's property, for need has made it common.'[20] In a contemporary context, Paul VI appealed to Aquinas to justify expropriation of large land holdings that were not being used to meet the needs of the poor and thus implicitly to argue that a free market in land is not a sufficient guarantor of justice. Land reform programmes in developing countries, for example, can call for government intervention in the market to assure that the needs of all are met.[21]

Centesimus Annus innovatively extends this argument from agricultural to industrial and post-industrial contexts. It is not only land and other natural resources that are created by God for the benefit of the whole of humanity. The 'universal destination of created goods' applies to human know-how and skill, for these human capacities have been created by God for the benefit of the whole human community. The resources that are the result of human intelligence and creativity ('know-how and technology') are not the purely private possession of anyone. Just as human beings are dependent on the natural resources of the created world to meet their needs, they are also dependent on the community for the nurturing and education that enable them to engage in economic innovation and entrepreneurship.[22] Thus the results of the use of entrepreneurial skills do not belong to the entrepreneur alone, since the skills have themselves been received in large part from the community. Entrepreneurs have a responsibility to put the results of this creativity at the service of the community. Ownership of the products of human labour and economic creativity becomes common in the face of human need just as it does with land and other natural resources. There are ethical limits to the operation of markets in both natural resources and in goods created by human innovation and initiative.

The results of efficient and productive markets, therefore, ought to be at the service of the community, especially those in need. This means the market should be organized to enable the vast numbers of people who are at present marginalized from it to become active market participants. So *Centesimus Annus* concludes that if ownership of physical capital or control of 'know-how' and 'skill' impedes the participation of others in this network of solidarity, it 'has no justification, and represents an abuse in the sight of God and man'.[23] Put positively, this means that the alternative to the failed Communist system is what the pope calls 'a society of free work, of enterprise and of participation'. This will be an economy in which the market is 'appropriately controlled by the forces of society and the State, so as to guarantee that the basic needs of the whole society are satisfied'.[24]

The distinction between civil society and the state is important to the Catholic tradition's approach to market regulation. The tradition's rejection of the state socialism of the former Communist bloc does not leave the free play of market forces as the only alternative. The principle of subsidiarity calls for the resolution of social problems at the level close to those affected by them. When communities are small or of intermediate size, they enable persons to act together, empowering them to shape public life and its larger social institutions such as the state and the economy.

Subsidiarity is thus a fundamentally anti-totalitarian principle. It is not, however, an anti-state principle that maintains that the government which governs least governs best. Rather, government 'should, by its very nature, provide help [*subsidium*] to members of the body social, it should never destroy or absorb them'.[25] It should intervene to the extent required by the demands of justice and in a way that preserves the vitality of the other communities that make up civil society. In Leo XIII's words, 'whenever the general interest of any particular class suffers, or is threatened with, evils which can in no other way be met, the public authority must step in to meet them'.[26]

Today this articulation of the legitimate role of government in the quest for justice needs to be reaffirmed, both in the West, where the outcome of the Cold War is a temptation to complacency, and in the East, where reaction to a statist past is a temptation to uncritical support for *laissez-faire* markets. The principle of subsidiarity, with its stress on the importance on the local, the small-scale and the particular, must be complemented by a kind of solidarity that is more universal in scope. In many countries and on the global stage, the real threat to the intermediary communities comes not from excessive state action but from the power of markets. *Centesimus Annus* raises a strong voice against this tendency towards domination by market forces: 'There are goods which by their very nature cannot and must not be bought and sold.'[27] For example, the dignity of working people, the survival of the poor and the greater participation of developing countries in the global economy are not commodities. So the dynamics of commodity-exchange are inadequate to secure justice in the provision of these goods. In the words of *Centesimus Annus*:

> The State must contribute to the achievement of these goals both directly and indirectly. Indirectly and according to the *principle of subsidiarity*, by creating favourable conditions for the free exercise of economic activity, which will lead to abundant opportunities for employment and sources of wealth. Directly and according to the *principle of solidarity*, by defending the weakest, by placing certain limits on the autonomy of the parties who determine working conditions, and by ensuring in every case the necessary minimum support for the unemployed worker.[28]

This provides a key to understanding what *Centesimus Annus* says about the welfare state or what it calls 'the social assistance state'. The pope notes that the range of state intervention to remedy 'forms of poverty and deprivation unworthy of the human person' has expanded in recent years. 'In some countries', he suggests, this has led to 'malfunctions and defects in the Social Assistance State', which are the result of 'an inadequate understanding of the principle of subsidiarity'. These defects are the sapping of human initiative and energy through excessive bureaucratization. State interventions to alleviate poverty, the pope says, are 'justified by urgent reasons touching the common good' (this is the principle of solidarity). But subsidiarity implies that such interventions are 'supplementary' to the primary source of economic welfare, viz. active participation in economic life through work. They are also supplementary to the direct assistance that, if possible, should be provided by families, neighbours and others who are closest to those in need.[29]

The pope's words are markedly similar to those written some years ago by the American economist Arthur Okun. Okun argued strongly for the freedom and efficiency of market economies and against the repression and inefficiency of centralized command economies. At the same time he stressed that commitment to the fundamental equality of all citizens sets limits on what can be bought and sold. This should put us on guard against 'the imperialism of the market's valuation', whose unchecked expansion would turn society into a 'giant vending machine that delivers anything and everything in return for the proper number of coins'. Other values – such as political rights of citizens, the basic conditions of survival, the bonds of affection in friendship and family, and the honour and recognition due to genuine human excellence – should not be up for sale. These other values, Okun says, 'are the glue that holds society together'.[30]

The protection of these values and the human communities in which they can be realized is a precondition for what John Paul II calls solidarity. To the extent that values of the market override them, human beings face 'increased isolation in a maze of relationships marked by destructive combativeness and estrangement'. If the market becomes the dominant organizing principle in society, we experience 'a reversal of means and ends' in which persons serve the laws of supply and demand rather than the other way round.[31]

The principle of subsidiarity demands that government be limited, but it is neither a libertarian principle nor an endorsement of the sort of neo-liberalism that is being newly discussed today. Nor, despite efforts to maintain the opposite, is it compatible with those forms of neo-conservatism that supported Reaganite and Thatcherite views of political economy. The government has an important role to play both in protecting the place of the market in society and simultaneously keeping the market in its place. Government intervention 'encourages, stimulates, regulates, supplements, and complements' the operation of the market, 'as the occasion requires and necessity demands'.[32] The 'juridical framework' for the market urged by *Centesimus Annus* is the means by which democratic government seeks to direct both the economy and civil society in ways that serve the common good. The Catholic tradition makes strong arguments for such a framework at a time when doing so is unpopular. This is perhaps the church's most important contribution to the debates about the future of market economies today.

Notes

1. *Centesimus Annus*, no. 42. English translations of the papal encyclicals and Vatican II documents cited here are found in David J. O'Brien and Thomas A. Shannon (eds.), *Catholic Social Thought: The Documentary Heritage*, Maryknoll, NY 1992.

2. Vatican Council II, *Gaudium et Spes* nos. 24 and 30, section titles.

3. *Centesimus Annus*, no. 24.

4. *Centesimus Annus*, nos. 32 and 34. See Max Stackhouse, 'John Paul on Ethics and the "New Capitalism"', *Christian Century*, 29 May-5 June 1991, 581.

5. *Centesimus Annus*, no. 33.

6. National Conference of Catholic Bishops (US), *Economic Justice for All*, Washington, DC 1986, no. 77.

7. *Centesimus Annus*, no. 33.

8. *Centesimus Annus*, no. 38.

9. *Centesimus Annus*, no. 26.

10. *Centesimus Annus*, no. 35.

11. *Centesimus Annus*, no. 42.

12. Leo XIII, *Rerum Novarum*, no. 2.

13. *Rerum Novarum*, nos. 28–34, 36–38.

14. *Centesimus Annus*, nos. 15 and 19.

15. *Gaudium et Spes*, Part I, chs. 1, 2, and 3.

16. See Milton Friedman, *Capitalism and Freedom*, Chicago 1962, 13.

17. John XXIII, *Mater et Magistra*, nos. 59–67.

18. *Centesimus Annus*, no. 32.

19. *Centesimus Annus*, nos. 32 and 43.

20. Thomas Aquinas, *Summa Theologiae*, II, II, q. 66, arts. 2 and 7.

21. Paul VI, *Populorum Progressio*, nos. 22–24.

22. See John Paul II, *Laborem Exercens*, no. 13.

23. *Centesimus Annus*, no. 43.

24. *Centesimus Annus*, no. 35. Emphasis in the original.

25. Pope Pius XI, *Quadragesimo Anno*, no. 79.

26. Leo XIII, *Rerum Novarum*, no. 28.

27. *Centesimus Annus*, no. 40.

28. *Centesimus Annus*, no. 15.

29. *Centesimus Annus*, no. 48.

30. Arthur M. Okun, *Equality and Efficiency: The Big Tradeoff*, Washington, DC 1975, 12–14. Okun's discussion has been elegantly elaborated and deepened in Michael Walzer, *Spheres of Justice: A Defense of Pluralism and Equality*, New York 1983.

31. *Centesimus Annus*, no. 41.

32. John XXIII, *Mater et Magistra*, no. 53; Pius XI, *Quadragesimo Anno*, no. 79.

A Positive Valuation of the Market in Ethical Perspective

Antonio Lattuada

The vast literature which has dealt with the market as a co-ordinating system of economic activity – from an ethical perspective – often has two main failings. The first is its clearly apologetic approach. Especially in the period of history in which the alternatives of a market economy and a planned central economy also represented two complex political, military, cultural and ideological systems, the choice for or against the market suddenly took on the character of an unavoidable choice between two opposing cultures, indeed between two opposing world-views. Hence the tendency towards 'propaganda', in which the passion for a legitimate cause often came before an intelligent perception of the complex questions posed by the modern economy.

The impracticability of the attempt to plan a modern economy from the centre has been definitively confirmed by the collapse of the Communist regimes of Eastern Europe. If in the new geopolitical context the apologetic approach to the market has evidently lost plausibility, another defect has often continued to afflict ethical reflection here, namely anachronism. To justify or to criticize or challenge the market economy, theses and commonplaces are repeated which – though they may have been relevant in the past – now scarcely correspond to the current reality of the modern economy, which is notoriously a process in continual and quite rapid evolution.

If we are to understand the problem of the morality of the market economy properly, it may be worth while remembering some distinctions currently used by economists. The main one is the distinction between the ideal market on the one hand and the concrete historical forms of the market which to a variable degree approximate to the ideal model on the other.

The ideal market: its advantages

It is well known that the earliest theories about the modern economy, first in the period of commercial capitalism and then from the beginning of industrial capitalism, could refer to a situation quite close to that of the 'ideal market' or 'perfect competition'. In such situations it was in fact possible to observe the surprising and almost magical correspondence between individual freedom and the common good, between pursuing a particular interest and the realization of the 'wealth of nations', between 'private vices' and 'public virtues'. In the historical conditions of this period the mechanism of prices in fact managed to co-ordinate automatically and in an optimal way the demand for goods and services expressed by the consumers and the production of them by businesses.

The list of conditions which constitute the situation of the ideal market has been given in different forms,[1] but among other things it provides that: 1. there shall be many sellers and buyers, none of whom has a substantial share of the market; 2. all the sellers and buyers are in a position to enter or leave the market freely; 3. all have complete information about the prices, quantities and quality of goods put on the market; 4. the costs and the benefits of production and use of goods exchanged fall entirely on those who buy or sell the goods, and not on 'outside' third parties.

In the presence of such conditions – in particular the first two define the situation of 'perfect competition' – the free market, in which each tries to maximize his own interest, automatically produces an economic and social asset which has features that are particularly noteworthy from an ethical perspective. More precisely, in such a method of organizing productive and distributive economic activity, the quantity of goods available and the prices attached to them tend spontaneously towards a 'point of equilibrium' at which the prices correspond simultaneously both to the value that the consumers put on the goods acquired and to the costs sustained by the sellers in producing them. In this way the moral demand of equity or justice is also realized, more precisely in the sense of the commutative justice for which each of the participants in the exchange receives the exact equivalent of what he gives.

Moreover the regime of perfect competition provides a stimulus towards the optimal efficiency of the productive system understood as the elimination of waste. The producers are in fact induced simply by the quest for profit to invest resources where consumer demand is high and to withdraw them from where it is low, introducing into the market what is in fact required by the needs of the consumers; they are also stimulated to reduce to the minimum the quantity of resources involved in the production of goods and to use the most efficient technology available for lowering costs, and at the same time required to contain their profits so as to keep pace with the competition of the other producers.

Finally, the market regime makes it possible to pursue such objectives as are morally relevant by safeguarding as well as possible the rights of the individual freedom of those involved. This is a particularly valuable advantage in the face of the growing specialization and division of tasks typical of a highly developed technological economy and hence of the corresponding need for co-ordination and integration.

The ideal market and its limits

There are thus substantial reasons of an ethical kind in favour of the choice of a system of market economy and, consequently, against the opposite alternative of a centrally governed economy. However, the limits or defects of the system are also known. First of all they relate to the same theoretical model of the ideal market which presupposes the condition of perfect competition. The advantages that this produces in terms of justice, efficiency for the common good and freedom in fact apply only to those who can participate in the exchanges of the market to the degree that they have the corresponding economic resources. By contrast, the needs and the demands of those who do not at present have an adequate purchasing power (children, the disabled, the sick, the old, etc., but also future generations) do not in principle have any influence on the market. So the market does not automatically provide for the 'common good', even in its 'ideal form', but only for the good of more or less numerous and fortunate groups of collectives which exist at present. In this sense its moral legitimacy is not justified in the light of a more comprehensive criterion of justice.

Furthermore the market, even in its ideal form, is structurally incapable of providing so-called public goods, or goods which by their nature are freely accessible even to those who do not contribute towards producing them or keeping them by paying the relevant costs. For this reason no private enterprise is obviously induced to bear the burden of them, even though they may be thought to be of essential importance. In fact some conditions which are necessary not only for the functioning of the market – the legal order or the road system for example – but even for the very survival of human beings and their quality of life, like the physical and cultural environment, have the nature of 'common goods'.

The real markets: the need for political control

The merely partial advantages indicated above arise only when the conditions which constitute the ideal market and in particular the regime of perfect competition prevail. By contrast the real markets, especially those of a technologically advanced and complex economy like the modern economy, never realize such conditions adequately, or at any rate do not do so spontaneously. The propensity of modern businesses to restrict the freedom of the markets and competition by the formation of monopolies, oligopolies and by explicit or implicit agreements aimed at 'programming' the quantities and prices of their products is well known.

By contrast, the same technical and economic complexity makes it virtually impossible for all the operators to have all the information to make a well-considered and therefore free choice. Average consumers today are not normally in a position to know all that they would need to know in order to choose the product best suited to their needs.

Furthermore – and this is an aspect which deserves special attention because of its specific moral implications – the needs for which the modern system of production makes satisfactory provision are now predominantly 'dynamic' needs; these are needs which are not rigidly or biologically predetermined but can be shaped through their predominantly psychological components. For this reason they are very much influenced by methods of public communication, which in their turn exercise an economic force. Thus the quality of the demand is not simply predefined in terms of economic initiative, as the model of the ideal market supposes, but can be orientated on the criteria or the interests which inspire this initiative. In a developing economy the logic of the market therefore risks producing the paradox that the complex of aims in respect of which the technical apparatus of production should pursue only an instrumental function is in reality determined by the apparatus itself.

Finally, the environmental crisis has shown at a macroscopic level how serious the phenomenon of 'negative externalities' is in the real markets. Relevant costs which often cannot even be quantified, for example in terms of the pollution and deterioration of the environment, the consumption of limited and non-renewable natural resources, damage to physical health because of working conditions and to mental health because of the restructurings made necessary by technological progress, do not exercise any influence on the mechanisms of the market and therefore on the determination of prices. But these costs are a charge on society, and usually on its weakest members, who do not have proportional benefits. The history of the trade union movement, which is indissolubly bound up with the development of the economic system of the market in industrialized countries, is an incontestable demonstration of the need for conscious provision of remedies to such defects in the free market.

If the market in its 'ideal' form already only partially realizes the values of justice, efficiency and freedom, and therefore needs to be integrated into a political project which seeks to remedy its objective limits, the need for such remedies is all the greater in the case of 'real' markets. This is first of all because the 'free market' conditions necessary for the production of the values indicated do not occur spontaneously. Rather, they call for interventions explicitly aimed at correcting the auto-suppressive tendencies to which the markets are continually exposed. Furthermore, because the dynamic character of the modern economy is based on technological innovation, it gives the system of production an exorbitant influence on shaping social and individual modes of life. If the ethical reasons expressed synthetically in the idea of the common good or the good life of society call for the formation and active promotion of a free market, at the same time they also require that this should be to some degree regulated and governed by non-mercantile criteria.

The alternative to the economic system of central planning is therefore not determined univocally. Rather, it allows the possibility of many forms of complex economic and social organization in which it is possible to assign a constitutive role to the market without submitting to its hegemony.[2] The role of the market would be supreme if citizens did not succeed in forming and publicly establishing 'demands' different from those which are already suggested to them as consumers by the system of production. The crisis of the welfare state or of the form taken by the state among Western nations above all during the 1970s must not simply mean the abandonment of the motives which inspired this political model. Rather, it should be the occasion for looking for other and more opportune ways of realizing these objectives. The political institution should not propose taking the place of civil society but rather should guarantee the necessary conditions for the latter, in its manifold articulations and expressions, including the task of 'governing' the market actively, or integrating it into a plan which is political and therefore has ethical characteristics. The first of these conditions is met by channels and forms of public communication which are not influenced by the market itself and are aimed at securing a common consensus to goals which are worthy and practicable for the life of society.

The contribution of recent 'business ethics'

One significant and promising phenomenon here is the renewed interest among one area of public opinion, above all in intellectual circles and even among entrepreneurs, in the ethical questions raised by the market economy. This is the complex of theoretical and practical contributions currently denoted by the term business ethics.[3] The history of this cultural movement is relatively brief. Only in fact since the middle of the 1970s, though quite rapidly, have initiatives of various kinds proliferated which have aimed at a treatment of business, or entrepreneurial activities aimed at making a profit in the context of a market economy, from a moral perspective. The conditions which have favoured this movement have also been complex. One relevant factor has been the development from as early as the 1930s of large corporations, or enterprises in which the figure of the entrepreneur and more generally of management, by virtue of the very structure of the business as a joint-stock company, progressively differs from that of the proprietor or those who provide the financial capital, taking on a relative professional autonomy. The interests which inspire the initiative and the entrepreneurial strategy no longer coincide with those of the proprietors, or do not consist solely nor even primarily in financial profit, but can be adapted to different aims (the development of the business itself, increase in prestige or power, social recognition, and so on).

On the other hand, the very increase in the power of businesses, made possible by their often enormous size, and in the increasingly sophisticated technology used for mass production, has contributed towards compromising the credibility of the business world in the eyes of widening sectors of society. From the 1970s onwards serious economic and financial scandals have increased in the USA, above all cases of corruption among representatives of the public administration, the payment of percentages to win contracts and gain positions of advantage in the market, the pollution of the environment (Bhopal, Seveso), collaboration with states with unjust political regimes, the marketing of foods and pharmaceutical products which are damaging to health, or insufficiently secure transportation, and so on.

The crisis of trust in relation to civil society and more generally the risks connected with the decline of local customs or cultures has led many business circles to seek to recover the moral credibility that has been compromised. This has given rise to a process of institutionalization of business ethics, or the implementation of structures and procedures aimed at preventing illegal or immoral behaviour in business itself. The most common forms of this institutionalization are the 'ethical codes' which publicly formalize the values and principal moral norms that the business means to observe, the 'ethical committees of directors' which involve the heads of the business in the work of applying moral standards, the ethics officer who is entrusted with implementing the directives of the ethical committee, programmes for the training and supervising all the staff of the business, and hot lines to allow free and constant communication on ethical questions internal to the business.

Academic and intellectual circles have also made an indispensable contribution to this programme. Philosophers and economists have shown growing interest in the study of business ethics. The number of courses in business ethics set up in universities and business schools and the textbooks used in connection with them are constantly increasing; there are also many specialized institutes or research centres which organize conventions or publish journals of business ethics.

One of the most significant and highly successful theoretical contributions of this research is the development of a new concept. Echoing the English term 'stockholder', i.e. the person who holds a share of the capital of a business, the term 'stakeholder' has been coined to denote all those whose interests or rights are in some way affected by the activity of a business. Obviously recourse to the term 'stakeholder' is not exhausted in a linguistic artifice, but aims to overcome the privatistic conception of the business which gives priority to the interest of the proprietor – or the maximization of profit – and instead to promote an approach which gives adequate recognition, with corresponding rights and duties, to the role of the varied subjects who in different ways play a part in the functioning of a business. Here, in addition to the shareholders, the managers at different levels, the dependent workers, the clients or consumers, the suppliers, the other rival businesses, the local community on which the business operates and the whole of civil society are stakeholders of the business. The use of the concept of stakeholder thus reflects a wider view of the business, presenting it as a broad network of relations which are often conflictual: a fair resolution of conflicts requires that no legitimate interest be arbitrarily ignored or undervalued, yet leaves space at times for different orders of priority.

The business ethics movement obviously shares in the problems which afflict any theories about ethics in our period, and in the impossibility of gaining a sufficiently specific cultural consensus over the basic criteria for moral values and thus for identifying causes which deserve commitment at a personal or public level. The heightened pluralism of opinions which characterizes the present situation and therefore ethical reflections easily leads even recent business ethics to withdraw to the level of procedural rules necessary for the peaceful negotiated settlement of conflicts over interests and values, objectives regarded as uncontroversial. Moreover this orientation for the most part characterizes both European and American business ethics and is probably one of the reasons for its lack of relevance in this cultural area even among those involved in the economy.

Despite such limits, business ethics makes a useful contribution to the development of an intelligent practical understanding of the modern market economy. It starts 'from below', or from problems of personal ethics (microethics) which arise every day within a productive organization in the context of a market economy. Then the perspective of personal ethics inevitably proves insufficient for an adequate solution to such problems, and calls for attention to be shifted to the structural conditions of business ethics: first of all the organization of the business itself (mesoethics) as the basic unit of the productive system, and then the organization of the economic order not only at a national level but, given the dynamics of the modern economy, also at an international level (macroethics). From the debate started on business ethics a Christian reflection on the modern economy could prove advantageous, and moreover could be a stimulating and determinative factor.

Translated by John Bowden

Notes

1. For a more analytical account see e.g. A. Buchanan, *Ethics, Efficiency and the Market*, Totowa 1985.
2. See e.g. A. Rich, *Wirtschaftsethik, Vol. II, Marktwirtschaft, Planwirtschaft, Weltwirtschaft aus sozialethischer Sicht*, Gütersloh 1990, which lists and analyses some possible different orders of the system of the market economy, e.g. capitalistic market economy, socialist market economy, Ota Sik's democratic human economy and the economy of the ecologically regulated market.
3. For an introduction to this see R. E. Freeman (ed.), *Business Ethics. The State of the Art*, Oxford and New York 1991.

The Market from the Ethical Viewpoint of Liberation Theology

Enrique Dussel

> 'Scripture says, "My house shall be a house of prayer";
> but you have made it a robbers' cave' (Luke 19.46).

The first codices of ethics known to humankind combine economic prescriptions with critical ones. For example, King Uruinimgina of Lagash (2352–43 BCE) included the following ethical-economic text in Law 27 of his *Legal Reform*: 'He freed and condoned the debts for those indebted families . . . who lived as debtors . . . He promised Ningirsu solemnly that he would never hand over the widow and orphan to the oppressor.'[1] In the same vein the Egyptian *Book of the Dead*, originating in the area of the sacred city of Memphis (going back some 5,000 years), also enunciates ethical-economic criteria: 'I did not impoverish a poor man in his goods . . . I made none suffer hunger . . . I added no [weight] to the measure on the scales. I did not falsify the weight on the scales . . . I placed no dyke in the way of running water . . . I did not rob with violence . . . I gave bread to the hungry, water to the thirsty; I dressed the naked and gave a boat to the shipwrecked.'[2] (In Jesus' discourse on the final judgment in Matthew 25.35–36, the ethical-critical requirements are in the following order: hunger, thirst, housing, clothing, sickness, prisoners; Isaiah 58.7 has: bread, housing, clothing – leaving out water. The *Book of the Dead* has: bread, water, clothing, boat [= house], changing the order of clothing and housing, but more complete than Isaiah. Could Jesus have taken his inspiration from this rather than from Isaiah? Elsewhere Jesus follows the order in the *Book of the Dead*: 'I bid you put away anxious thoughts about food and drink to keep you alive, and clothes to cover your body' [Matt. 6.25]. Engels follows the same order, which is really more logical, as clothing must come before housing: 'What serves for food, clothing, housing.'[3])

These highly critical criteria – still valid today – have a material, economic, critical meaning. So, if we take the six stages of moral consciousness analysed by Lawrence Kohlberg,[4] we can match them with six degrees of 'ethical-critical' consciousness. Thus at a very low formal level of moral development, alongside magic and very primitive still pre-conventional myths, we already find material ethical-critical criteria and principles which are highly-developed – even in relation to conventional modernity. How is this possible? Because in the Egyptian-Mesopotamian world there was a very early material-critical consciousness, on which the Hebrew prophets drew and which they developed to its full extent; the same can be said of Jesus of Nazareth.[5]

I. The origin of the ethical-theological theory of the modern market

The modern science of economics, definitively formulated in the eighteenth century, stems from ethics and arises as the theological solution to a problem. Book V of the *Nicomachean Ethics*,[6] on justice, gave rise to the medieval and renaissance commentaries *De jure et justitia*, as we know, and through them to modern economics. Justice is the virtue of a tendency (called *appetitus* by the Latins). Pre-Kantian modern ethics would still be a material ethics of impulses and virtues. Also, there is nothing strange in Aristotle telling us that, 'we can use a shoe, for example, to put on our feet (use value) or as an article of exchange (trade value)'.[7] Money, on the other hand, which serves only for trading, has 'no value' in itself.[8] Money presupposes the existence of the 'market', the traditional 'space' in which the trade in the products of human work is carried out, which is pre-historic: the clans of the Paleolithic era were already trading their products. Although the 'market' was a social and economic 'place' recognized in all pre-modern ethics, 'money' – which is a formal instrument of exchange only, having purely 'trade value', especially in the case of its accumulation through avarice – has been the object of continual condemnation. For Aristotle, 'money . . . does not correspond to anything by nature': it is perverse. And of course, for Jesus, 'You cannot serve God and money' (Matt. 6.24) – a Gospel phrase that appears frequently in the works of Marx.[9] The condemnation applies even more strongly to loans at interest: see Deuteronomy 23.20–21. Calvin reinterpreted this text, allowing Christians to lend at interest to other Christians, a doctrine John Knox carried to Scottish Presbyterianism. It is therefore not strange to find, years later, Adam Smith occupying the chair of moral philosophy in Knox's Edinburgh![10] Contradicting a tradition going back thousands of years, modern 'market theory' then arose as the solution to an ethical-theological dispute in enlightened Presbyterian Scotland, with its Calvinist tradition. In his *Fable of the Bees* (1705), Bernard Mandeville had cynically confronted – without much hope of success – the hypocritical moralizing position of many members of 'commercial society' by stating that 'private vices', such as egoism, the self-interest of the nascent bourgeoisie, could bring 'public benefit' – the wealth of the nation, the elimination of poverty through paying wages to the wretched, and so on. Put this way, the formula could not be accepted by traditional Christian moralists, or by the 'common sense' of a semi-feudal population, which would not accept such contradictions of its deepest convictions.

It was Adam Smith who effectively solved the problem, even though many others had preceded him and nearly all of what he wrote in *The Theory of Moral Sentiments*[11] had been expressed before. Starting from a scientific theory derived from Newton[12] (Smith had studied astronomy, physics and other sciences, with particular admiration for Newton), the whole ambit of human behaviour, moved by passions or sentiments, should be explained by means of certain non-intentional regularities that govern society as the natural laws do nature. (He uses the following argument: 1. Someone can through the sentiment of sympathy put himself in the place of another [there is an actor and a spectator]; 2. Then someone places himself in front of another and a spectator [so there are now an actor, a patient and a spectator]); 3. Finally the actor imagines himself to be his own spectator: this 'spectator' is his own conscience, which from 'impartial spectator' changes into an authentic 'transcendental spectator' – here largely anticipating Kant himself. This universal 'moral conscience' which each individual carries within himself is the same as the presence of the omniscient Stoic God who, present in every individual, reveals to us the 'harmony' of a system of behaviour, morality, virtues: 'For Smith, the supreme tribunal is total and absolute perfection, which can be none other than the tribunal of God, the Great judge, the Omniscient author of Nature.')[13] And since Christians cannot simply accept the cynicism of Mandeville – 'All public spirit, therefore, all preference of public to private interest, is, according to him, a mere cheat and imposition upon mankind; and that human virtue which is so much boasted of, and which is the occasion of so much emulation among men, is the mere offspring of flattery begot upon pride'[14] – the discovery (in the manner of a real scientific-social 'invention') is made that the market is the 'space' (as though it were a laboratory) in which a spectacular metamorphosis is produced. This is somehow necessary while unperceived by every individual conscience, in the sense of not being decided by any individual, so non-intentional – which gives an absolute guarantee to the order, 'regularity', or legality that is its effect. This is the self-interest of each particular individual, no longer seen simply as the vice of egoism, which struggles chaotically, irrationally and disorderedly for its own ends. (It is understandable – and even revolutionary – that, faced with the apathy of a feudal society simply following established paths and promoting conformism and lack of creativity by attacking egoism, the nascent – and so critical – bourgeoisie should justify 'the selfish and original passions of human nature [which appear] to be of vastly more importance'. This of course leads rapidly to criticism of the 'melancholy' of many moralists who exaggerate 'commiseration for those miseries which we never saw'. Smith recommends concentrating on what really motivates human beings – self-interest, and not commiseration with the sufferings of the alien poor.[15]) But this self-interest produces public benefit or love of neighbour as its 'effect', thanks to the intervention of a provident God, who regulates the whole like a clock – the Newtonian self-referring machine in the hands of the divine clockmaker. (Speaking of the Stoics, whom he admires and follows, Smith writes: 'A wise man never complains of the destiny of Providence, nor thinks the universe in confusion when he is out of order. He does not look upon himself as a whole . . . He enters, if I may say so, into the sentiments of that divine Being, and considers himself as an atom . . . Riches or poverty, pleasure or pain, health or sickness, all is alike.' And: 'According to Zeno, the founder of Stoical doctrine, every animal was by nature recommended to its own care, and was endowed with the principle of self-love, that it might endeavour to preserve, not only its existence, but all the different parts of its nature.'[16] So self-interest has been reconciled with common good; self-love with love of neighbour. The way to a science of economics was open, and Smith developed it on the classical lines of the moral philosophy of his time, moving from natural theology through ethics, in *The Theory of Moral Sentiments* (1759) to a consideration of justice and government in *Lectures on Jurisprudence* (1763), developed over ten years (1766–76) into *An Inquiry into the Nature and Causes of the Wealth of Nations*. In this he famously claimed that we generally look in vain for the help we seek from others by appealing to their benevolence, and would do better to appeal to their self-love, to make them see that it is to their advantage to do what one is asking of them: 'Give me that which I want, and you shall have that which you want.' It is not the tradesman's benevolence that provides us with food, but his consideration of his own interest: we invoke not his humanitarian sentiments, but his self-love.[17]

Ultimately, this is a theology that reconciles the opposites:[18] it is the provident 'hand of God' that draws, necessarily and non-intentionally, a rational order (the market, the 'space' of universality) out of the irrational chaos or disorder (of individual self-interest). Individuals do all they can to promote their domestic interests, and thereby find themselves necessarily contributing to maximizing the income of society as a whole – the formal outcome of a 'means and ends' instrumentality, its 'effect'. As a general rule, no one sets out (the action is non-intentional) to advance the public interest; nor does anyone know (again, the non-consciousness of the effect produced, even though this is still necessary, as we have seen) to what extent he is promoting it. In such cases, we are guided by an invisible hand to promote an end that had not entered into our calculations. It is the very non-intentionality that epistemologically allows the 'science' of economics more surely to achieve a 'regularity' that approximates it to Newtonian physics.[19]

So far we are still on the level of economic 'necessity', through divine intervention, so at the natural theology stage of the classical argument this is a theological economics. Smith concludes, ethico-theologically, that there is nothing wrong for society in public interest not entering into its calculations. (Here he is arguing against the traditional ethics in which the self-understanding of and responsibility for an action were ethical constituents of it. He is now showing that economic structures exist beyond explicit intentionality.) By promoting their self-interest, people advance the interest of society in a more effective manner than they would have done if it had entered into their calculations. (Smith uses the 'efficacy' argument here, but at the same time is critical of feudal, traditional, moralizing society, which rejects the nascent 'commercial society' of his time. He is thereby providing an ethical-theological basis for the bourgeoisie in its critical, prophetic, revolutionary phase. The devastating 'effects' of these non-intentional consequences had yet to be seen, and it was to be left to Engels to show intentional ethical commiseration with the suffering of their victims, in his magnificent *The Situation of the Working Class in England*.) Rulers who seek to direct individuals as to how they should employ their private capital are taking on an 'impossible task'.[20]

Here we have a clear and deliberate outline of the market economy model and of the 'impossibility' of trying to regulate it. The 'Law of the Market' – as a necessary ontological regulator – requires, in this theory, that the market be left to regulate itself through its own non-intentional structures – a 'cybernetic system', as we would call it today[21] – which are both necessary and best, speaking ethico-theologically. To touch this so perfect and extremely complicated 'clock' is pride: only the 'hand of God', the perfect clockmaker, can interfere. Humility means attending to the very reality of the market.[22] This state of affairs leads, after the event, to the formulation of Hume's so-called 'natural fallacy' – the feudal, moralistic, apparent 'ought to be' is replaced by the effective 'being' of the market. What concerns us is the 'being' (of the self-interest of the market);

the 'ought to be' remains up in the air and is no longer necessary. In effect, 'being' now has its own ethics.

II. Ethics as market 'function'

Friedrich von Hayek, of the Austrian school,[23] can be taken as representative of the most radical neo-liberal economic tradition today. Adam Smith has undergone deep changes. In the first place, Smith is a critical economist, critical of feudalism and mercantilism; Hayek is a conservative economist, against the 'constructivist rationalism' of the social democratic or Keynesian welfare state and Soviet central planning. In the second place, while Smith sees the market as regulated by 'the hand of God', with Hayek it has become a condition for the ontological possibility of the sufficient knowledge of everything it needs to operate – to 'offer' what is on offer and to 'prefer' what is demanded. Faced with the human impossibility of possessing perfect divine omniscience – the individual's humble recognition of the cognitive limits of his own finite reason – of the infinite complexity of the world, the market – through the mechanism of fully free competition without monopoly or coercion (an absolute condition) – provides us with sufficient knowledge through 'prices':[24] 'Although the science of economics has duly analysed the phenomenon of division of labour . . . it has not devoted a similar effort to the problem of the fragmentation of knowledge.'[25]

Partial human knowledge, thanks to the monetary calculation of price in the – purely formal – 'market system', is now the chief player in any 'possible reasoning'. 'Market order' is a natural, spontaneous, non-intentional system, with no need of voluntary intervention. The market system, however, needs a basis for its operation: this is the currently dominant moral order, which provides the customs and institutions on which the market mechanisms operate, its basic rules being: respect for private property, recognition of the effective freedom of every participant,[26] obligation to honour stipulated deals, honesty in observing the rules of competition, discipline in saving, and so on. (Norms such as altruism, solidarity, fellowship or equality are expressly excluded: 'An order in which all treated their fellows as themselves would lead to a world in which few would have the possibility of multiplying and fructifying.')[27] 'We live in a civilized society, because we have come to assume, in a non-intentional manner, certain inherited habits of a fundamentally moral character . . . Acceptance of moral norms transmitted by tradition – norms on which the market rests – is what allows us to generate and utilize a greater volume of information and resources than a centrally-planned economy could place at the disposal of the community.'[28]

Purely individual morality is dissolved in this 'wide order' – Hegel's *Sittlichkeit*, or Lévinas' *totalité*. Hayek sets out to rebuild the history of the current moral order of the present-day bourgeois market, the product of a centuries-long natural evolution. The paradox is that he rationally bases (argues) this current morality, taking the 'survival of humanity' as its rationale: 'The debate between the market order and the socialist is a question that decisively affects the very survival of the human species. The assumption by society of socialist recommendations in questions of ethics would imply the disappearance of a large part of the population and the pauperization of the remainder.'[29] (He fails to see that these are precisely the 'effects' of an untrammelled market economy!)

The efficacy, operability, of the competitive market system is demonstrated by the very survival of the members of present-day civilization. Life is the major premise of the argument. In this way 'current bourgeois morality' – in Hayek's extreme traditional and conservative sense – is not an *a posteriori* expression that seeks to justify the market – as was done by H. B. Acton, for example, who in Chapter 3 of his *The Moral of the Market*, entitled 'The Ethics of Competition', tried to justify competition; Hayek on the other hand shows the (ontological) moral 'condition of possibility' of competition (*a priori*). (This was the sense in which Marx said that economics, 'despite its worldly and pleasurable appearance, is a true moral science, the most moral of all the sciences. Self-denial, renunciation of life and of all human needs is its basic dogma. The less you eat and drink, the less liquor you buy, the less you go to the theatre, to balls, to the tavern . . . the more you save, the greater becomes your treasure that neither moth nor rust devour, your capital.')[30] Hayek proposes a naturalist ontology, which makes the market and competition the normative, non-intentional, ethical frame of reference, beyond the reach of any sort of criticism – the conservative concept of 'tradition', which Karl Popper also proposes. (Ricardo Gómez, in a strictly epistemological refutation, comments: 'Society is only the sum total of the individuals that make it up, linked to one another especially by a system of homogeneous traditions . . . Hayek is right to state that a free society is a society of traditional links. Whence both for him and for Popper . . . trying to change it radically is irrational, since it would imply among other things abandoning the genuinely free society.'[31]) Ultimately, this is a tautology: starting from the current bourgeois morality and the formal pre-existence of the market, it goes on to deduce its normative foundations – still always argued *a priori* and defined as basic norms. Then, on the basis of these – which, as I have indicated, were deduced from the market – it claims to provide an ontological-ethical and historical-evolutionary foundation for this same market. This is what I have called a 'functional ethic'; it has its theologies and the 'social teaching' of some churches, equally functional.[32] This functional ethic is deduced from: (a) a functional social science – in this case an extreme one, belonging to a neo-liberal, conservative economics, in which the 'logic of the global market' of itself most effectively assures the survival of the human race; (b) a really existing capitalist system.

III. Prophetic criticism of the market

How should a critical, or liberation, theology proceed in the face of formulations of this sort, with their pretension to scientific objectivity, inevitability, and economic common sense? It should have recourse to the critical criterion of negation and materiality, as Horkheimer notes: 'What traditional theory [meaning neo-liberal economics] allows simply as current, its positive role [Hayek's 'positivity' of the market system is 'affirmation of the ruling ethnicity'] in a functioning society . . . is questioned by critical thought. The aim this sets itself, a situation based on reason, is founded on the actual misery of the present . . . The theory outlined [both 'negative criticism' of the market system and 'positive construction of alternatives'] by critical thought does not operate for the benefit of an existing situation.'[33] Horkheimer is here speaking of two situations: that of the current order (the market, in this case), and that of the future based on a 'praxis of liberation'. Or, as the founder of the Marburg School, the Orthodox Jew Hermann Cohen, writes: 'The prophets were not philosophers, but they were politicians . . . The poor became for them the symbol of human suffering . . . Thus, their God becomes the God of the poor. The social insight of the prophets recognizes in the poor the symptomatic sign of the sickness of the State.'[34] Or again, as a message from the Zapatista Army for National Liberation reads in a Mexican daily:

> The eldest of the elders of our peoples spoke to us words that came from afar, from when our lives were not, from when our voice was silent. And the truth walked in the words of the eldest of the elders of our people. And we learned from their words
>   that the long night of suffering [suffering being the 'sign' of material negativity, of living corporeality as the starting point of criticism] of our peoples came from the hands and words of the powerful,
>   that our wretchedness was wealth for a few,
>   that on the bones and dust of our ancestors and our children a house had been built for the powerful,
>   and that our footstep could not enter this house,

and that the abundance of its table was filled from the hollow of our stomachs,
and that its luxuries were born of our poverty,
and that the strength of its roofs and walls was raised on the weakness of our bodies,
and that the health that filled its spaces came from our death,
and that the wisdom that dwelt there was nourished on our ignorance,
that the peace that ruled there was war for our peoples . . . [35]

Such statements, like those of the biblical prophets, are redolent of a critical logic that derives always from affirmation of life for human beings as 'flesh' – Hebrew *basar*, Greek *sarx*, which is not the mere 'body' – as the criterion of truth – of judgments on reality, of science, of theology. Justice is always linked to life: 'Surely life is more than food, the body more than clothes' (Matt. 6.26); life is the criterion of truth: 'The Word . . . was alive with his life, and that life was the light [= truth] of men' (John 1.1–4); 'I am the way, the truth and the life' (John 14.6); life for, or the full satisfaction of, the poor is the 'kingdom of God' (Luke 6.20–24). Life is the criterion of truth integrated in the norms, actions, institutions or ethical systems; it is the content of what is good: 'Today I offer you the choice of life and good, or death and evil' (Deut. 30.15). What kills (death) is contained in a 'false', one-sided pronouncement by those who hold power; this has death-dealing instrumental 'efficacy': what it effects is evil – in its norms, actions, institutions or ethical systems, such as Hayek's market.[36] (My forthcoming work on the ethics of liberation mentions a third criterion of demarcation: the first distinguishes science from what is not science; the second distinguishes between natural and human, or social sciences; this third distinguishes functional from critical human or social sciences.[37] In some ways the Popper-Adorno debate pointed to some aspects of this 'third' criterion, but it did so confusedly.[38] Adorno – like the Frankfurt School in general – confused these three criteria in the debate between 1. analytical or positivist thought [of the instrumental reason] and 2. dialectical-critical thought. The ethics of discourse – in losing the negativity–materiality of ethics – cannot even posit the theme of what is 'critical'. We need to distinguish between: (*a*) dialectical thought as understanding, and (*b*) scientific social thought as explanation; but also between (*c*) 'functional' social sciences [such as in von Hayek, which can in some cases be dialectical] and (*d*) 'critical' social sciences [which have to be dialectical, but also have other requirements]. Furthermore, 'critical' human or social sciences need to be distinguished from (*e*) 'critical' philosophy [without confusing the two into an ambiguous 'critical theory']. Finally, and applying these epistemological distinctions to the area of theology, (*f*) critical theology, such as liberation theology, which is not a 'functional' theology – as are most of the current theologies of the 'universal religions' – now has to posit with epistemological precision the whole question of this 'third criterion of delimitation'.[39])

Life has to be considered in its sacramental materiality; 'Take this and eat; this is my body [*basar*]' (Matt. 26.26); 'I was hungry and you gave me food' (Matt. 25.35). This is the first material or universal ethical principle: every ethical subject is obliged (deontic principle) to make the content of every norm, action, institution or system of ethics (*Sittlichkeit*) promote the production, reproduction or development of the life of every human being in community, the building-up of the kingdom of God. The content of the pronouncement will then be true. The 'application' of this material universal principle requires a second, formal moral principle, which can be stated thus: every ethical subject is morally obliged to recognize as equal and to promote the symmetrical participation of every human being in his or her life (as a member of the kingdom of God) and therefore has to make an option in his or her argument and community. The consensus reached will then be valid. (This cannot be done, as Peter Ulrich proposes, through constructing an epistemology of the science of economics on discursive reasoning. He criticizes utilitarian economics, but fails to reconstruct a practical-material economic theory, since in the end he proposes only a discursive economic theory – that of the communicating community of economists – but not the constructive economic theory of the production, reproduction, and development of the life of every human being through means of communitarian, practical-productive economic relationships.[40]) Finally, the true and valid mediation needs a third principle, obliging us to do what is possible to do – unlike anarchists, who try to carry out what is impossible. And only when we carry out what is in practice true, valid, and possible will our norms, actions, institutions and systems of ethics be good. Theologically, this is a stage in building the kingdom of God.

What happens empirically or historically – using Popper and Hayek's arguments of the impossibility of 'perfect planning' – is that no economic system can – unfortunately – fail to produce victims as an unintended effect. Only a perfect system – empirically impossible – would produce no victims (For Hayek, although perfect competition is a model – leaving aside the inconsistency here, since if it is 'perfect' there can be no competition, either logically or empirically – it introduces to the empirical market a 'tendency' toward equilibrium, which cannot be demonstrated scientifically. This 'effect' of the market, equilibrium [a secularized version of Adam Smith's harmony through the Hand of God] acts, in the market, as a perfect system: that is, its negative effects – such as the dire poverty of the majority of human beings at the present time – are not products of any imbalance in the market, but of a lack of more market. We are here in the realm of metaphysics, in the worst sense of the word; this is an 'unfalsifiable' [as Popper terms it] ideological proposition, 'immunized' against any empirical rebuttal. In theology this is called idolatry; Marx called it fetishism; in epistemology it is false science.[41]) Smith observed cynically that in a civilized society only the shortage of food among the lower orders could limit the multiplication of the human race, and this could be brought about only by destroying many of the children born to fertile couples.[42] (He is arguing against slavery, that the labour of free man will always come out cheaper in the long run than that of slaves, since the 'frugality and careful attention of the poor' [!] is naturally found in the free.)

His cynical argumentation is directed against the society of his day, and so is critical and even revolutionary in its context, but his same reasoning applied today would show that it is cheaper to let the free poor in Bangladesh or the southern Sahara die than to try to save them from starvation or AIDS. Hayek hints at the same sort of argument when he writes that there will always be those perturbed by 'some effects of the market', and when, after showing the 'wonders' of the system, he claims that 'even in the most calamitous times, nine out of ten [persons] will see their hopes realized'.[43] But what if the situation were virtually the inverse – that today one person out of ten sees his or her hopes realized? And what if the market system were to produce, as an unintended effect, a desperate poverty for most of the human race and – now – a growing percentage of poor in the central capitalist countries? As it is impossible for there to be no 'poor' (the economic 'victims'), their presence can be tolerated when they are a minority or their situation is tolerable. But what happens when they become the majority and their situation becomes intolerable, that is, when the wealth of a few can no longer be cosmetically hidden in the face of the mortal misery of the poorest – as the Zapatista text from Chiapas showed?

When this happens, critical economic theory becomes necessary for a critical and realist theology. We shall have to find a 'scientific' basis for any 'explanation' of the 'causes' of the material negativity of the victims. (This would be a social science as a 'programme of scientific investigation' in the manner of Latakos, but of course using criteria of 'scientificity' developed critically and not the standard criteria used by Latakos himself: these, being very narrow and reductive, are too easily applied as ill-defined scientific demands and used to deduce that, for example, psychoanalysis, Marxist economic analysis, or – I would add – Paulo Freire's pedagogy of the oppressed, are not scientific. Such scientific discourses do not, evidently, meet the criteria of the functional sciences, but they do meet those of critical science, which starts from an ethical option, siding with the victims as the condition of a practical possibility of a 'critical' science. All this would lead us very far off, but we absolutely have to start the discussion, since this 'third' criterion has not yet been introduced into the epistemology of the philosophy of science as a criterion of 'demarcation'.[44]) In other words: we have to find rational arguments for the why of widespread poverty. There is a forceful text that explicitly defines what I shall henceforth call the 'third criterion of demarcation' in epistemology. Mark Marx's words carefully:

> It was clear that, since the same real development gave the bourgeois economy [what I have called 'functional social science'] its implacable expression, that is: the contradiction between the growing wealth of the nation in England and the growing penury of the workers; and since, furthermore, these contradictions were given, in the theory of Ricardo and others, a theoretically self-evident, though unconscious expression, it was natural for those thinkers who took the side of the proletariat to seize on the contradiction already made clear by them. Work is the only source of trade value and the only active creator of use value. So you say. But, on the other hand, you also state that capital is everything and the worker is nothing or simply a cost of producing capital. You contradict yourselves. Capital is no more than a swindle perpetrated on the worker. Work is everything.[45]

(The workers were the victims Marx visualized, but today we could formulate the contradiction within the market process as being the contradiction between the growing wealth of the 'central' capitalist countries and the growing penury of those on the 'periphery'. And Ricardo's 'unconsciousness' implies the unintended effects of the capitalist system.) These lines express the 'third criterion of demarcation' to which I have been referring. Marx also saw that it applied on the world scale; that, in the global market, not only individual capitalists but nations themselves could trade continually with one another while deriving unequal benefits from this trade, if not as unequal as in the dealings between capitalist and worker.[46] In Marx's 'programme of scientific inquiry', his concern was to 'explain the cause' of poverty: he called its structural cause 'surplus value' – value produced in 'overtime' and not paid for in wages; human life turned into an unpaid object and so stolen from the worker. This shows us the 'logic' of critical social science, what critical theology needs for its own discourse. Today I am more concerned with the linkage between the penury of the peripheral nations (their peoples, ethnicities, groups and classes) and the question of 'competition' among nations' capital, which allows the 'transfer' of value (surplus value) from one nation to another. Globalization has not proceeded so far as to blur national boundaries.

This means that, because it denies the possibility of promotion of life for the human subject, the norm, action or institution – here Hayek's 'market' – is interpreted theologically as the sin of injustice, since it is a denial of the kingdom of God in each human being, through the death of the poor. So an ethical-theological judgment can be pronounced – through analytical-critical means – on market theory, on its rules, its logic, and its supposed ethic.

The market, as defined by neo-classical and neo-liberal economists, is a formally auto-poietic, self-referrent and abstract system (like the 'L language' in Tarski's semantics or Luhmann's 'system'), whose only purpose is the reproduction of capital, within the framework of the market and dealing only in 'prices': it has no 'work-value' doctrine with which to measure anthropology and economics against ethics. The lives of human beings have no relevance whatsoever for such 'formal systems' – which have no content. 'Survival' is a topic, but only as an apology to hide the horrible unintentional effects, which no supposed 'balance' can prevent. What exists in practice is an appalling imbalance.[47]

So, the affirmation of life shows us that this is what is denied to the victims (the poor and unemployed in both peripheral and central capitalism): factual judgments or formal pronouncements (instrumental or dialectical-ontological in nature) are now judged as false, in that they fail to reproduce life; invalid, in that those affected have not participated in the decisions that victimize them; and ineffectual, since the efficacy of the market is not practicable reproduction of life for the majorities: it is ineffectual for life. The norms, actions, institutions or ethical systems that are the unintentional fruit of the market, as formulated by Hayek – its logic – contains the evil and injustice proper to those who kill: 'See . . . death and evil' (Deut. 30.15).

This leads us on to three further ethical principles: 4. the ethical-critical principle that obliges us to criticize the market system from its victims; 5. the consensual formal principle that obliges us to organize symmetrical participation for the victims – through the new critical social and political movements: ecological, feminist, workers' rights, Third World, and so on; and 6. the liberation principle that obliges us really to deconstruct the negativities – or norms, actions, institutions or ethical systems – and practically construct the new bodies needed – the complex stages of a liberation process.

Practical-material reasoning can then compare the ends to which the market as described by Hayek tends and judge them from the three positive ethical criteria (life; symmetrical participation; practicability) and – only now – launch its negative ethical 'judgment', deduced from the positive ethical criteria of the Last Judgment: 'I was hungry and you gave me food'

(Matt. 25.35). These negative ethical judgments (on 'hunger' and the like), which are normative pronouncements, are not primarily 'value judgments', as Rudolf Carnap or Alfred Ayer thought. The values are borne by norms, actions, institutions, and ethical systems insofar as they are mediations for the promotion of human life. The values do not found the ethics. Ethics does not consist essentially in subjective or individual approval or condemnation, but in judgments of universal facts: 'John is hungry because he has no wages (work) in the competitive labour market.' This is judging a fact! From this judgment of fact we deduce, contrary to Hume's badly-named 'natural fallacy',[48] that, on principle (and not considering specific cases but taking a universal view), 'I must give John food, or he will die without my help!' Emmanuel Levinas has shown us why we are 'responsible-for-the-Other', because in community and solidarity his death is the anticipation of our death; those who kill are committing suicide, since they are initiating or perpetuating a 'logic of negation of life' that will eventually bring about their own death – as a Latin American proverb puts it; *El que ha hierro mata, a hierro muere*, 'Kill with steel, die from steel'.

Translated by Paul Burns

Notes

1. See F. Lara Peinado and F. Lara González (eds.), *Los primeros códigos de la humanidad*, Madrid 1994, 24–5.
2. 'The Book of the Dead', ch. 125, in ibid., 202–9.
3. Prologue to 'The Origin of the Family', in *WEB*, Vol. 21, Berlin 1981, 27–8.
4. See L. Kohlberg, *Essays on Moral Development*, Vol. 1, Cambridge, Mass. 1981–2; L. Kohlberg and A. Colby, *The Measurement of Moral Judgment*, Vols. 1–2, Cambridge, Mass. 1987; J. Habermas, commentary in *Moralbewusstsein und kommunikatives Handeln*, Frankfurt 1983, 127ff. I deal with the critical criterion in my forthcoming *Etica de la liberación*, chs. 4 and 5.
5. *Etica* (n. 4), historical introduction and ch. 4 on 'critical ethics'.
6. 1129 a 1ff.
7. *Politics*, 1, 3; 1257 a 8–9.
8. Ibid., 1257 b 13.
9. 1257 b 12; see my *Las metáforas teológicas de Marx*, Estella 1993, 200ff., 'A central biblical text'.
10. Ibid., 139ff., 'Death in Deuteronomy: the Birth of Capital'.
11. *The Glasgow Edition of the Works and Correspondence of Adam Smith*, Vol. 1, Indianapolis 1987; see G. Gutiérrez, *Etica y Economia*, Univ. Iberoamericana, Mexico City 1996 (unpublished Master's thesis).
12. See 'A History of Astronomy' and other researches on similar subjects, in *Glasgow Edition* (n. 11), Vol. 3, *Essays on Philosophical Subjects*, 1980, 31ff.
13. Gutiérrez, *Etica y Economia* (n. 11), 29.

14. Smith, *Glasgow Edition* (n. 11), Vol. 7, 309.
15. Ibid., Vol. 3, 135, 139.
16. Ibid., 276; Vol. 7, 272.
17. *Wealth of Nations*, Book 1, ch. 2.
18. See A. T. van Leeuwen, 'Economic religion', Ch. 3 of *De nacht van het Kapitaal. Door het oerwoud van de economie naar de bronnen van de burgerlijke religie*, Nijmegen 1984, 310ff.
19. *Wealth of Nations*, Book 4, ch. 2.
20. *The Situation of the Working Class in England*, in *MEW*, Vol. 2, 225ff.
21. See N. Luhmann, 'Wirtschaft als soziales System', in K.-E. Schenk (ed.), *Systemanalyse in den Wirtschafts- und Socialwissenschaften*, Berlin 1971, 136–71; id., *Soziale Systeme. Grundriss einer allgemeinen Theorie*, Frankfurt 1984.
22. See F. Hinkelammert, *Cultura de la esperanza y sociedad sin exclusión*, San José 1995, and (with H. Assmann), *A idolatria do mercado. Ensaio sobre Economia y Teologia*, Petrópolis 1989.
23. See Various, *La Escuela Austriaca de Economía*, Mexico City 1989.
24. See the 'pencil' example in Hayek's popularizer, Milton Friedman, *Free to Choose*, New York 1979, 3ff. on 'The Power of Market'; id., *Capitalism and Freedom*, Chicago 1982.
25. F. von Hayek, *Derecho, legislación y libertad*, Madrid 1985, 40; on the whole question of Hayek's ethics, see Gutiérrez's *Etica y Economia* (n. 11).
26. Of Hayek's works, see *The Road of Serfdom*, Chicago 1972; and esp. *Los fundamentos de la libertad*, Madrid 1975, Vols. 1–2.
27. *Los fundamentos* (n. 26) 44.
28. F. von Hayek, *La fatal arrogancia. Los errores del socialismo*, Madrid 1990, 33–4.
29. Ibid., 35.
30. H. B. Acton, *The Moral of the Market*, London 1971, Ch. 3 on 'The Ethics of Competition'; Marx, *Mans.* 44, III, in *MEW*, Vol. 1, 549.
31. See R. Gómez, *Neoliberalismo y seudociencia*, Buenos Aires 1996, 170–1.
32. E. Dussel, *Ethics and Community*, Tunbridge Wells and Maryknoll, NY 1988, Ch. 19, 'The Gospel and the Social Teaching of the Church', 205–18.
33. M Horkheimer, *Traditionelle und kritische Theorie*, Frankfurt [4]1970, 35.
34. H. Cohen, *Religion of Reason out of the Sources of Judaism*, New York 1972, 23.
35. 'Once more we enter history', in *La Jornada*, Mexico City, 22 February 1994, 8.
36. See such texts as Deut. 5.19; 17.24; Lev. 5.21–23; Jer. 22.16; Hos. 6.6; also *Ethics and Community* (n. 32 above), ch. 1.
37. *Etica de la liberación* (n. 4), ch. 5.3. On the second criterion, see H.-G. Gadamer, *Truth and Method*, London [2]1981; G. H. von Wright, *Explanation and Understanding*, Ithaca 1971; K.-O. Apel, *Understanding and Explanation*, Cambridge, Mass. 1984.
38. See T. Adorno, K. Popper, J. Dahrendorf and H. Habermas (eds.), *Der Poitivismusstreit in der deutschen Soziologie*, Berlin 1969.
39. Ch. 6 of my forthcoming *Etica* (n. 4) takes a completely different approach from that based on Althusser as adopted in, e.g., C. Boff, *Teologia do politico e suas mediaçoes*, Petrópolis 1978.
40. P. Ulrich, *Transformation der ökonomischen Vernunft*, Bern 1993, 171ff.
41. See Gómez, *Neoliberalismo y Seudociencia* (n. 31 above).
42. *Wealth of Nations*, Book 1, ch. 8.
43. Hayek, *Fatal arrogancia* (n. 28), 142.

44. See Apel, *Explanation and Understanding*, and von Wright, *Understanding and Explanation* (n. 37).

45. Marx, *Mans.* 61–63, Notebook XIV, in *MEW*, 1979, 1390.

46. *Grundrisse*, Notebook VII, in *Grundrisse der Kritik der politische Ökonomie*, Berlin 1974; see my 'Marx's Economic Manuscripts of 1861–63 and the "Concept" of Dependency', 1990.

47. On the imbalance caused in the name of market 'equilibrium' see F. Hinkelammert, *Crítica a la razón utópica*, San José 1984, Ch. 2, on 'The Inconsistency of the General Theory of Equilibrium', 67ff.

48. Refuted in ch. 1 of my forthcoming *Etica* (n. 4).

IV · The Market and Some Challenges of the Contemporary World

The Free Market Economy and the Crisis of the Welfare State

Marciano Vidal

One of the major implications of the free-market, or neo-liberal, brand of economic system is the crisis into which it has plunged the welfare state. This brand of economic policy, which seeks to cut back social benefits, is creating serious problems for the personal, family and social well-being of large sectors of society, with those in the weakest economic positions suffering the worst consequences.

Faced with this situation, we need to ask: 'What are the most equitable criteria? What is the most effective solution? So I shall try to set out, simply and schematically: 1. the history and crisis of the welfare state; 2. the criteria that should guide government social policy; 3. a proposal for a social pact based on the value of solidarity, or the common good, as a positive (and not negative) successor to the welfare state.

I. The welfare state: its history and crisis

1. Genesis and features of the welfare state

One can speak of a welfare state in a very broad sense to refer to the most general social benefits, such as health insurance or public education up to a certain age. In this sense, there was a welfare state in the nineteenth century, at least in some countries. In fact, the term 'welfare state' originated in the model of social security created by Bismarck in Germany in 1883.

More precisely, however, the welfare state came into existence after the Second World War. Economic theorists faced up to the problems of the 'faults' from which the free-market system suffered, shown in most spectacular fashion by the Wall Street crash of 1929. It was John Maynard Keynes who produced the most brilliant and convincing defence of the need for state intervention through increased public spending to guarantee stable economic growth.

In the wake of Keynes' theories, the states that emerged renewed from the Second World War embraced the welfare option. Social Democrats, Christian Democrats and Liberals made a clear choice of the welfare state. Through interventionist measures, they gradually developed a form of society in which social security payments were guaranteed, generalizing a series of services in connection with education, health, unemployment, pensions and so on. In the 1940s the United Kingdom spearheaded this movement with the publication of the Beveridge Report in 1942. France and Germany followed with more nuanced approaches. Then the Scandinavian countries, headed by Sweden, took the model to its furthest stage of development. The rest of the European countries followed to a greater (as in Austria) or lesser degree, and the model spread to most of the developed countries worldwide.

The features that defined the welfare state had four basic characteristics;

1. *Full employment*. The labour market provided full employment. The number of unemployed was generally less than 3% of the working population. Security of employment was achieved through labour agreements that assured individual and family stability.

2. *Social security*. This had two characteristics: breadth and universality. It tended to include all citizens (universality) and to extend to ever-increasing aspects of social life (breadth): health insurance, accident insurance, unemployment benefit, pensions for all, and so on.

3. *Free public education*. The educational system stretched from nursery school to university. Education was free up to secondary level and tended to be assisted at higher levels through state or local scholarships for those who had the required levels of attainment but lacked the economic means.

4. *Social policy understood as redistributory*. The aim was not merely to palliate or redress scandalous inequalities, but also and primarily to favour a redistribution of wealth. Social policies were the instruments of this redistribution. The working of the welfare state raised the level of satisfaction in both individual and social life. Optimism and euphoria were translated into a more stale and egalitarian society. One result of this was a balanced population growth.

2. The crisis of the welfare state

The crisis of 1973 – most evident in the oil crisis, but with broader underlying causes and consequences, still needing more detailed study – marked a decisive shift in the concept of the state and the way society is organized. The cycle begun after the Second World War was brought to an end and a new one opened. In Europe the social democrat model was overthrown. Keynesianism lost its currency in economic theory. The neo-liberal conservative offensive was launched, aided by the collapse of 'real socialism' (Soviet communism).

Each of these factors had its own significance, but all converged on the same end: a change of model in the way the state was structured. During the decades of the 1970s and 1980s, the welfare state went through a deep and broad crisis. The causes of this crisis are complex and varied, but its main aspects (causes and effects together) can be noted:

1. *The disappearance of full employment.* Work became a scarce resource. New forms of employment appeared: short-term, 'hire and fire', part-time, self-employment, irregular, black economy. Employment precariousness brought obvious consequences: workers' powers decreased, along with cohesion among wage-earners; employer-employee relations tilted in favour of the employers, reducing the rights of employees and producing a more submissive attitude among them. Technological advances (with the concomitant need for re-training operatives) worsened the labour market, both numerically and qualitatively, with unskilled operatives becoming marginalized and the cost of a skilled labour-force increasing.

2. *State financial limits.* The welfare state was based on its financial capacity. But when expenditure rose on account of increased needs and tax revenues were reduced, the state became insolvent. Budget deficits rose beyond the level of what was tolerable. This brought cuts in public spending and, as a result, the overthrow of the welfare-state model.

3. *A change in basic values.* Concomitantly with social and economic transformations, a fundamental shift in the axiological system took place. 'Suspicions' of excessive bureaucracy, of the excessive amounts spent on social benefits, of over-egalitarian projects, began to be expressed. Doubts about the 'universalization' of particular social benefits surfaced. The values of competitiveness, of private initiative, of individual freedom, were extolled as a counterpart. The viability of 'privatization' and suspicion of anything that could be labelled 'socialization' became generally accepted.

Behind the crisis of the welfare state lurks a confrontation between differing models of society and of human life in general. What is clear is that, while in the three decades from the 1940s to the 1960s an egalitarian model of life predominated, the neo-liberal or free-market model has seen a resurgence in the last three decades of the century. Among the values involved in this confrontation between models of society, that of the common good has to be placed in the first rank. In my view, the egalitarian model makes a greater commitment to the common good than the free-market one. For that reason, I hold that we have to opt for a successor to the welfare state on the following lines:

—not supplanting it with its opposite, the free market state;

—not undertaking a nostalgic, last-ditch defence of the welfare state we know, as brought about in the decades following the Second World War;

—rather making it develop in a spirit of solidarity, correcting its faults and adapting it to new historical circumstances.

These are the criteria I put forward in the following section.

II. Criteria to guide government exercise of social policy

Very different stances can be adopted towards the crisis of the welfare state. One is to take free-market attitudes to a radical extreme, producing a market economy by virtually dogmatic means. Another is to live nostalgic-ally ensconced in the dream of a social state that might have been the solution to the problems of all its citizens, above all the least privileged. I believe that the most clear-sighted stance takes account of the new situation and tries to guide it into producing the positive dynamics of the welfare state while cancelling the excesses that reduced its effectiveness. This needs guiding criteria, which I attempt to set out in the three following sub-sections:

1. 'No' to the 'benefit state'

The first criterion: the 'benefit state' is not the solution. Rather than elaborate reasons, I should like to quote a considered passage from the encyclical *Centesimus annus* in which the limits of state benefits are pointed out:

> In recent years a vast increase in this type of intervention has taken place, which has in a way brought about the formation of a new kind of State, the 'Welfare State'. This evolution has come about in certain States in order to provide a more adequate response to many needs and deficiencies, trying to remedy forms of poverty and privation unworthy of human beings. Nevertheless, excesses and abuses have not been lacking and these, especially in recent years, have provoked harsh criticisms of this Welfare State, regarded as a 'benefit State'. Deficien-cies and abuses in this arise from a defective understanding of the duties proper to the State. In this sphere the *principle of subsidiarity* should

also be respected. A social structure of higher order should not interfere in the internal life of a social group of lower order, depriving it of its rightful responsibilities, but should rather support it in the event of need and help it to co-ordinate its actions with those of the other components of society with a view to the common good (cf. *Quadragesimo anno* 1).

By intervening directly and taking responsibility from society, the 'benefit State' produces a loss of human energies and an excessive increase in public bodies, dominated by bureaucratic logic rather than a concern to serve its clients, with an enormous increase in costs. In effect, it seems that those who are closest to needs or to the needy can better understand such needs and succeed in satisfying them. Furthermore, a certain type of needs often requires a response that is not only material, but can uncover its deeper human aspect. We also need to think of the situation of refugees and emigrants, of old people and the sick, and of all those others in need of help, such as drug addicts: all these are persons who can be helped effectively only by those who offer them, besides the necessary care, sincerely fraternal support (*CA* 48).

2. *Necessary state intervention*

Second criterion: by reason of the principle of solidarity, the state has to continue to intervene. This intervention has to be planned and executed for the sake of the common good of the whole of society and especially in view of the rights of its weakest members. The encyclical *Centesimus annus*, in no way inclined to collectivism and still less to statism, nevertheless points to the need for state intervention. Fields in which this is needed in the present situation are:

The institutional, juridical and political framework. The state has the duty to uphold a juridical framework to oversee the social actions of individuals and groups. In direct reference to the economy, John Paul II indicates that:

Economic activity, particularly the market economy, cannot develop within an institutional, juridical and political vacuum. On the contrary, it supposes a security guaranteeing individual freedom and property, besides a stable monetary system and efficient public services. The first duty of the State is, then, that of guaranteeing that those who work and produce can enjoy the fruits of their work and, therefore, feel stimulated to perform it efficiently and honestly. Lack of security, together with corruption of public offices and the proliferation of improper sources of enrichment and easy rewards, based on illegal or purely speculative activities, is one of the main obstacles to development and economic order (*CA* 48).

Interventions in situations that affect the well-being of society as a whole. In the economic field, the state has a 'duty of harmonizing and directing development'. More specifically, it has the right and the duty to intervene 'when particular monopoly situations create hindrances or obstacles to development' (*CA* 48). This criterion can, by analogy, be applied to areas of society other than the economy: health, education, culture, and so on.

Substitutive functions

The State can exercise substitutive functions, in exceptional circumstances, when social structures or business systems are too weak or just being formed, and unable to supply such functions themselves. Such substitutive interventions, justified by urgent needs affecting the common good, should whenever possible be limited in time, so as not in the long run to deprive such social structures or business systems of their responsibilities and not to broaden the ambit of state intervention excessively so as to damage both economic and civil liberties (*CA* 48).

Defence and protection of 'common goods'

It is the duty of the State to provide for the defence and protection of common goods such as the natural environment and the human environment, whose safeguarding cannot be assured by plain market forces. Just as in the days of the old capitalism the State had the duty to defend the basic rights of labour, so in the new capitalism the State and society have the duty to defend collective goods, which, among other things, constitute the only framework within which it is possible for all to pursue their individual aims legitimately (*CA* 40).

Limiting the 'idolatry' and voraciousness of the market. The state today provides a limit to the exuberant ramifications of the market. In connection with the necessary protection of common goods, John Paul II notes:

Here there is a fresh limit to the market: there exist collective and qualitative needs that cannot be satisfied through market forces; there are important human demands that escape their logic; there are goods that, by their nature, cannot and must not be bought or sold. Of course, market forces offer some definite advantages: they help, among other things, to make better use of resources; they favour trade in produce and, above all, give primacy to personal will and preferences as expressed in contracts made with other persons. Nevertheless, they carry the risk of an 'idolatry' of the market, which ignores the existence of goods that, by their nature, are not and cannot be pure merchandise (*CA* 40).

3. Social strategies for channelling solidarity

From the two preceding criteria we can deduce the need to propose social strategies that will channel the spirit of solidarity. I propose simply two:

1. *More insistence on 'society' than on 'the state'.* We need to correct the deviations into which the welfare state has fallen. Critical examination of this experience suggests that excessive bureaucratization of solidarity is not good, nor is it good to provide social spending without at the same time activating the abilities of its recipients. These two exaggerations in the functioning of the welfare state should steer social intervention for the common good more towards 'society' than towards 'the state'. It is the recipients who should initiate their own services, thereby giving rise to an involved and not merely a receptive society. This, needless to say, does not suppose the elimination of government; but it does mean that the apparatus of the state should have a subsidiary role, leaving the leading role to society itself.

2. *Social protection not opposed to competitiveness.* Free-market critics of the present system of social security point to the danger that it reduces and even cancels out the competitiveness that is needed. For this not to happen, we need to correct the distortions introduced into a social system based on the quasi-magical principle that all benefits must come down from above. As this affects the world of work, it would seem necessary to reduce the level of claims and accept limits to the policy of redistrubution so that competitiveness and stability can be maintained.

III. From the 'welfare state' to the 'solidarity state'

1. A social contract of solidarity

If we are to move beyond the crisis of the welfare state in a positive way, we need to introduce the value of solidarity into the social contract.[1] Several specialists in social philosophy maintain that the social contract of modern times, based fundamentally on the principles of freedom and equality (the social contract of free and equal human beings), has to be reformulated with the introduction of the third principle of the French Revolution, fraternity/solidarity. This principle takes account of the inevitable asymmetry of the human condition and responds to it with solidarity, which means treating those who are unequal (through having less) in an unequal manner (by showing them preference).

The ethical principle of solidarity expresses a moral value that society has to embody if it seeks to be a society ordered according to justice:

–As a principle, it 'rules' society in its moral dynamism; it sets it an ideal goal; it stimulates it and guides it on its road to this goal; it provides it with the criterion for discerning how far and in what way it has progressed towards or deviated from the ideal.

—As an ethical principle, solidarity is understood in its axiological sense: that is, as having value and more specifically moral value. Its central aspect is that of an axiological principle. Nevertheless, as a principle that regulates social life, it has to have embodiments in other spheres of norms besides moral ones. The ethical principle of solidarity by its nature has specific outcomes for:

channels of a juridical nature, by means of adjustments to constitutional norms, to laws of a general or organic nature, and to more specific norms deriving from them;

options of a political nature, by means of establishing an adequate framework of institutions and actions to make the value of solidarity viable in actual circumstances.

Furthermore, the principle of solidarity has multiple applications to social life: it is a principle of political organization; it is a criterion for labour and trade union economic bargaining; it is a requirement for the judicial system. All these applications have their basis and origin in the general ethical meaning of solidarity.

It has to be said that we are dealing with a principle that still lacks proper analysis. Of the three principles of the French Revolution (liberty, equality, fraternity), the first two have been developed in social theory and now form guiding principles in social life, having succeeded in being incorporated in the constitutions of many states. Yet the ideal of fraternity understood here as solidarity has not had the same success up to now. It is time to revindicate this ideal of fraternity or solidarity as one of the basic principles of social life.

2. The meaning of the principle of solidarity

The principle of solidarity overcomes isolationist individualism (latent in the principle of *amour propre*) and closed collectivism (as justified by the principle of 'co-operation'). Genuine solidarity formulates a nobler ideal for social life: that of the tendency toward ethical equality of all individuals, while taking account of the situation of asymmetry in which the least favoured individuals and groups find themselves.

There are two features that define the principle of solidarity and make up the two great axiological requirements of a society guided by that principle:

1. *The radicalization of 'sociability'*. A macro-requirement of the principle of solidarity is to make people, through social institutions and structures, come together not only as a group of free and equal subjects for the sake of self-regarding exchange, but also from a certain sympathy and

out of the real desire to collaborate in order to satisfy the interests of all the components of the group (world, country, social group).

In this sense, the principle of solidarity radicalizes the value of sociability: this is not only the fruit of the contract between free and equal subjects having a value in themselves (as ethical subjects, ends in themselves), but also the result of the ethical consideration of all subjects as bearers of a deeper mutual dependence that makes them feel themselves to be co-sharers in the situation of all.

The principle of solidarity expounds and embodies sociability in its strong sense. This is why the symbolism of this strong sociability is the 'family', and why the term 'solidarity' is often interchanged with the term 'fraternity'.

2. *An axiological preference for the weakest.* Precisely through uncovering these strong senses of sociability, the principle of solidarity introduces into social life (on the international, national and social group levels) the ethical consideration of 'the unequal'. Starting from the realization that social relations are 'asymmetrical', solidarity shows which side one has placed oneself on in order to make unjust inequalities disappear and inevitable inequalities be taken into account through a preference that emphasizes the axiological value of the weakest. Understood in this way, solidarity is the principle that guides asymmetrical social relationships ethically. It is a basic axiological principle of a social life that claims to be authentically 'human' in fullness of empathy and co-operation.

For this principle of solidarity to become reality, society has to be seen as incorporating a solidarity contract. The theory of 'social contract', an understanding still extant in our days, is fundamentally based on consideration of human persons as free (autonomous) and equal (with a symmetrical equality). This consideration needs to be extended with: as free and equal within the asymmetrical condition of human life. This asymmetrical condition is assumed morally through the principle of solidarity. As can be seen, this is a matter of recovering the third, forgotten principle of the French Revolution: fraternity, which today is better translated by the term solidarity. In order to adopt this principle of solidarity, we have to radicalize the social contract by turning it also into a solidarity contract. Only through such an understanding of the social contract can the present crisis of the Welfare State be overcome, but in a positive (or progressive), not negative (or regressive) form.

Translated by Paul Burns

Notes

1. For a development of the theme introduced in this section, I refer to my recent study, M. Vidal, *Para comprender la Solidaridad, virtud y principio ético*, Estella, 1996.

The Market and Ecology

Iring Fetscher

The discovery of the dynamic effect of the creation of a free market for goods, services and persons by Adam Smith fascinated his contemporaries. Whereas hitherto market relations had been constricted within the framework of conventional prices and traditions, from now on all producers and consumers were to act on the basis of a rational calculation of their own interests. In this way, as Adam Smith could demonstrate in his *magnum opus, Inquiry into the Causes of the Wealth of Nations* (1776), in a very short time the mass of products and thus the wealth of a whole economy would multiply. Competition among those involved in the market would ensure that as much as possible was produced as cheaply as possible. The mechanism of competition would compel each individual producer to calculate rationally. The rise in living standards would no longer be dependent on the moral behaviour of those involved in the market but only on the rational calculation of their own interests.

> It is not from the benevolence of the butcher, the brewer, or the baker that we expect our dinner, but from their regard to their own interest. We address ourselves, not to their humanity, but to their self-love, and never talk to them of our own necessities but of their advantages (Book I, Chapter II).

The most effective means of making products cheap was – as Smith observed – the progressive distribution of work. It meant that ever less complicated activities were required from individual producers and that increasingly machines could be incorporated into the production process. Right at the beginning of his work Smith states in a very matter-of-fact way, but also firmly, that distributing work and making it cheaper and more simple would damage the development of a large part of society. In contrast to the theory of the genetic difference between human gifts which arose much later, Smith assumed that human beings come into the world with relatively equal capabilities, but as a result of their later activities develop in extremely different ways. Even such gross differences as those between a philosopher and a simple street worker could be derived less from their innate properties than from education and later activity (ibid.).

Now as a progressive distribution of work is the necessary consequence of the market society, it will also be the case that a large number of people will lag behind in their intellectual and emotional development. In Book V, Part III, Article II, 'Of the Expenses of the Institutions for the Education of Youth', Smith therefore arrives at the result that the government – in its own interest and that of society – is obliged to correct this development by measures for state education.

> In the progress of the division of labour, the employment of the far greater part of those who live by labour, that is of the great body of the people, comes to be confined to a few very simple operations; frequently to one or two. But the understanding of the greater part of men is necessarily formed by their ordinary employments. The man whose whole life is spent in performing a few simple operations, of which the effects, too, are perhaps always the same, or very nearly the same, has no occasion to exert his understanding, or to exercise his invention, in finding out expedients for removing difficulties which never occur. He naturally loses therefore the habit of such exertion, and generally becomes as stupid and ignorant as it is possible for a human creature to become. The torpor of his mind renders him not only incapable of relishing or bearing a part in any rational conversation, but of conceiving any generous, noble or tender sentiment, and consequently of forming any just judgment concerning many even of the ordinary duties of private life. Of the great and extensive interests of his country he is altogether incapable of judging; and unless very particular pains have been taken to render him otherwise, he is equally incapable of defending his country in war.[1]

The government should therefore guarantee at least a minimum of basic knowledge and skills also for these persons who are put at a disadvantage by their monotonous and tedious work.

Adam Smith is quite clear that the enormous increase in industrial production brings considerable disadvantages for the great majority of workers who have no property. But he evidently assumes that this price has to be paid for the economic advancement of the 'wealth of nations'.

Adam Smith is equally clear that human beings by no means have an 'equal' or even approximately equal economic starting point. We even find him saying:

> Civil Government, so far as it is instituted for the security of property,

is, in reality, instituted for the defence of the rich against the poor, or of those who have some property against those who have none at all (Book IV, Part II, Expenses of Justice).[2]

In view of these sober statements by Smith it remains astonishing that he expects a completely free market gradually to level out the great differences in wealth. He explicitly assumes the same thing for the relationship between the British mother country and India. His optimistic assumption is that within the foreseeable future the free market will level out these extremely large differences. However, he hardly assumed such an automatic levelling out for the majority of the population with no property, and his description of the government as an instrument for protecting the rich against the poor at least suggests that in this respect his thought was very down-to-earth.

Nowadays, given the development of techniques of production and communication since then, one can object to Smith's pessimistic description of the way in which monotonous work dulls people by pointing out that these conditions have improved, at least for a large part of the work-force. However, it is still appropriate to note that the dynamic of the development of the market economy did not intend such improvements, but merely accepts and furthers them to the degree that they are in its own interest.

Another effect of market competition which goes beyond the frontiers of individual states was the introduction of monocultures, above all in the colonies but also in countries like Ireland. The potato monoculture, which first brought advantages to the poor country, led – in connection with failed harvest and disease – to famine and the pressure towards mass immigration. Proneness to disease and attacks by parasites increases tremendously with the introduction of monocultures and brings with it considerable danger to the lands or regions concerned. The Irish famine in the 1840s was a first gross case of ecological damage by monocultures through the principle of maximizing the market economy – though it could not have been described in that way at the time.

The negative consequences of agriculture programmed to a maximization of production also became clear in the USA at an early stage. Industrialized agriculture with the use of artificial fertilizers, insecticides and herbicides often leads in a relatively short period to a loss of fertility in the soil. However, such a development was not regarded as tragic as long as it was possible to open up new areas to agriculture. In our century the devastating consequences of agriculture and forestry programmed exclusively on more intensive and cheaper production are becoming most evident in the annihilation of the tropical rain forests, the existence of which is indispensable for the equilibrium of the climate of whole areas of the earth. I shall be returning to the ecological problems of colonial monocultures and the destruction of the tropical rain forests in connection with the concept of 'sustainable development'.

First of all we need to consider the way in which the industrial market economy exhausts nature and puts a burden on it. As early as 1845, in his report on *The Situation of the Working Class in England*, Frederick Engels described the damage to health in industrial towns and especially in the areas where the workers lived. In 1878 he documented the ecological damage done by an uncontrolled development in a market economy, namely the pollution of water by the textile industry.

> The prime need of steam engines and the main need of almost all branches of the great industry is relatively pure water. But the industrial town turns all water into stinking cesspools. So although concentration in towns is the basic condition for capitalist production, every individual industrial capitalist enterprise strives to get away from the towns that it has necessarily produced and moves into the country. This process can be studied in detail in the areas devoted to the textile industry in Lancashire and Yorkshire; the capitalistic industry constantly creates new large towns by progressively moving from the town to the country. It is the same in areas devoted to the metal industry, where causes which are partially different have the same effect.[3]

Since water, like air, as a rule does not cost the individual business anything, on the basis of the principle of the minimization of costs it is motivated to pollute the water and the air heedlessly. The same thing is also true of a whole economy, at least as long as free trade prevails. If the use of water purifiers and air filters, etc., is required in a city by legal regulations, there is a danger that industrial concerns based there will be shifted to cities which do not have such restrictions. Only the high investment costs for big business offer a certain amount of help here towards the possibility of regional measures to protect the environment. In general, however, the 'globalization' which has come about through the extension of free world trade and the free movement of money, investments and labour is making any corrective of the devastating and extremely wasteful consequences of the market economy motivated by democratic politics considerably more difficult to achieve.

The market is certainly an ideal way of raising production and quality by the use of self-interest, but it is completely insensitive to long-term damage done to nature and human beings who are workers and consumers. This damage need not necessarily be connected with the market economy, but it is always done when the relevant compulsory regulations – which can be legally enforced – are not laid down. In a free world economy the overall conditions need to be established internationally. As the world is still a long way away from that, major environmental catastrophes are to be expected before an appropriate agreement is arrived at.

The prime cause of the indifference of the market economy both to the consequences for individual producers, which Adam Smith already noted, and to the effects on the natural basis of life, is that the market economy thinks purely in business terms. The only connection taken into account by pure market economists is the connection between the mechanism of competition and the appearance of more and cheaper (and if possible also improved) products on the market. Moreover this development seems to be unlimited, and the vast increase in productivity simply over the last fifty years seems to confirm the impression. For a long time the limited quantity of natural resources (e.g. coal, oil and gas) and the increasing damage, especially to the atmosphere, were not noted.

Karl Marx, who could not have recognized the significance of the environmental problem as clearly as we can today, nevertheless saw very clearly in *Das Kapital* the damage done both by industrial agriculture and by industry itself.

In modern agriculture, as in the urban industries, the increased productiveness and quantity of the labour set in motion are bought at the cost of laying waste and consuming by disease labour-power itself. Moreover, all progress in capitalistic agriculture is a progress in the art, not only of robbing the labourer, but of robbing the earth; all progress in increasing the fertility of the earth for a given time, is a progress towards ruining the lasting sources of that fertility. The more a country starts its development on the foundation of modern industry, the more rapid is this process of destruction. Capitalist production, therefore, develops technology, and the combining together of various processes into a social whole, only by sapping the original sources of all wealth: the earth and the workers.[4]

The logic of short-term maximization of utility for every individual concern is in no way contradicted by this negative effect. Long-term calculations necessarily lie beyond the horizon of an economic order whose nature is an unpredictable dynamic – and a purely individualistic approach. Karl Marx only rarely formulated moral demands. But in connection with the destructive effect of a pure capitalistic market economy on nature and human beings he once formulated a notion which unexpectedly show points of contact with a posthumous text of Walter Benjamin's. In Volume III of *Das Kapital*, Marx states:

From the point of view of a higher economic form of society, the private ownership of the globe on the part of some individuals will appear quite as absurd as the private ownership of one man by another. Even a whole society, a nation, or even all societies together, are not the owners of the globe. They are only its possessors, its users, and they have to hand it down to the coming generations in an improved condition, like good fathers of families.[5]

In a posthumous fragment 'On the Category of Justice', Walter Benjamin made some remarks which could supplement and confirm Marx's ideas:

Any commodity, being limited in the order of time and space, acquires the character of a possession as an expression of its transitoriness. But *possession*, as being *caught up in the same finitude, is always unjust*. Therefore no order of possession of whatever kind can lead to justice. Rather, justice lies in the *condition of a good which cannot be possession*. This alone is the good through which goods cease to be possessions. In the concept of society (understood in socialist terms) one attempts to give the good a possessor who does away with its character as possession. Every socialist or communist theory falls short of its goal because the claim of the individual extends to every good.

This also applies – we must understand Benjamin to mean – to the collective subject, society or socialized humanity. 'Justice' – according to Benjamin's counter-thesis – 'is not concerned with the right of the person [or the collective] to possessions but with *that of the good to be a good.*' 'Justice is the *effort to make the world the supreme good.*' 'Justice can ultimately only be *a condition of the world, or a condition of God.*'

The petition in the Lord's Prayer, 'Lead us not into temptation, but deliver us from evil, thy kingdom come', is a petition for justice, for a just state of the world.[6]

What Benjamin calls possession is described by Marx more precisely as property. Common to both is the notion that the earth makes a claim on our behaviour. That here the right of future generations to life must be taken into account is also in accord with Benjamin's thesis.

The thesis of this article is not that the market is harmful in every respect, but that a completely uncontrolled market economy and what it produces have a series of consequences which need conscious correction. The fact that Adam Smith already saw the need for government action here should make it clear that this is not an 'anti-market economy dogma', but is concerned with the conditions within which alone the healthy effects of the market and competition can be ensured. Without these conditions the economic system would ultimately destroy itself – as Fred Hirsch has demonstrated. The concept through which the whole range of changes in our economic activity – both in production and consumption – which are needed becomes clear is that of 'sustainable development', a term which has already been around for some time. I want to conclude my remarks by sketching this out.

The most important addition that this new concept makes to earlier ecological thought is the introduction of a consideration of the ever-increasing economic inequalities in the world. If we start from the fact that each individual and each people should have a roughly equal 'environmental space' in the world, it becomes clear to what degree life-styles – the exhaustion and the pollution of nature – must be lowered by the highly-industrialized states so that this aim can be achieved (at least to some extent).

By 'environmental space' the authors of the book *Sustainable Netherlands* (the Dutch Friends of the Earth) and other studies which work with this concept understand the space that the inhabitant of a particular country claims for the satisfaction of his or her needs – living, eating, drinking, travelling. It is not easy to calculate this space. For example the assumption that a country like the Netherlands can be 'self-sufficient' in meat is deceptive because here the agricultural surface needed overseas for providing food for the cattle in the Netherlands is not taken into account. So in addition to the fields and pastures needed in the Netherlands, these overseas countries need to be taken into account. The same is true of other commodities: imported wood for furniture, imported raw materials of all kinds, etc. Fuel is another factor to be taken into account: aviation fuel, diesel oil, etc., which are needed for transporting goods from distant countries.

As the resources on earth for these fuels are also limited, with a just and equitable distribution the Western Europeans, North Americans and Japanese would be due very much less fuel than they actually claim for themselves. Only if the usage and waste of natural materials of all kinds is to some degree reduced and the pollution of air, water and earth suffered equally by all the inhabitants of the earth can there be talk of 'sustainable development'. In Germany the term is connected with forestry and indicates that no more wood must be cut than grows from new plantings. How drastic the restrictions would have to be if the goal of sustainable development were to be achieved emerges from a calculation of the reduction in the consumption of exotic fruits (because of the high transport costs) and the necessary renunciation of long-distance travel which the authors of *Sustainable Netherlands* have suggested. For example, a single flight to the Caribbean would use up the fuel allowance for one person for twenty years. Such examples are only illustrations, and if different climatic and cultural starting points were taken into account they would certainly come out differently; nevertheless, the concept of environmental space and its just distribution is an important one in specifying the new conditions necessary for the market economy to survive. The theological notion which appears in the fragment by Walter Benjamin, that justice is a 'state of the world', could be a starting-point for a theological argument in relation both to a world-wide sharing of burdens and also to the sense of a principle of responsibility for generations in the future.

Translated by John Bowden

Notes

1. George Adam Smith, *The Wealth of Nations*, The World's Classics, Vol. II, 417.
2. Ibid., 341.
3. *Marx-Engels Werke*, Berlin 1962, Vol. 20, 275f.
4. Karl Marx, *Das Kapital I, Marx-Engels Werke*, Vol. 23, 529f.
5. Marx, *Das Kapital III, Mark-Engels Werke*, Vol. 25, 784.
6. Quoted from Walter Benjamin, 'Notizen zu einer Arbeit über die Kategorie der Gerechtigkeit', in *Frankfurter Adorno-Blätter IV*, Edition text and kritik 1995, 26f.

The 'Market' and the Inviolability of Human Dignity in the Perspective of Biomedical Technology

Dietmar Mieth

1. Open, modern society is both an economic society and a constitutional society. In both these aggregate states society lives in tension with itself. Granted, the primacy of politics over the economy is analogous to the primacy of the constitution, but the reality is more complex. For example, one can regard the termination of pregnancy both in terms of legal permissibility (i.e. more than not carrying a legal penalty) and in terms of its acceptance by society as a victory of the economic society over the constitutional society. Women are progressively being integrated as individual subjects of the economy, and the price which the constitution requires for this – namely equal treatment on the one hand and unequal treatment and solidarity in respect of their reproductive role on the other – is not being paid by society. Because it does not provide the solidarity which is really necessary to prevent situations of conflict over pregnancy, the constitution has to yield here. But we shoud learn something from this process.[1]

2. One of the ethical principles which support the constitutions of legally ordered states is that some goods are not at its disposal: they may not become commodities or be commercialized. This applies, for example, to human dignity and to parts of the human body (against trade in organs and tissues). The planned or already legal inclusion of the cells of the human body (e.g. genes) among goods that can be traded is therefore rightly being disputed. The issue here is one of patenting,[2] i.e. the privilege of excluding others from procedures, genetic information and products. The proposal that parts of the human body should be patented, although bio-chemically they are identical with the original cells, which is already law in some countries, is a sign that the hopes of their use on the

new biotechnological market are exerting increasing pressure on constitutional principles. Another example is the pressure from abroad and at home on the strict federal German legislation which protects embryos. We shall be discussing this further.

3. The economic society wants a free market, shaped by the forces of supply and demand. However, freedom does not mean that the market is unregulated, and this unrealistic misunderstanding must be ruled out immediately. Anyone who really wants freedom needs regulation, so that freedom can also develop – e.g. in the sense of freedom from competition or rights of equal access. Where deregulation of the market is called for in the name of freedom – either of business or research – one must ask: Is the issue freedom *of the* market, privileges *on the* market, or freedom *from the* market? Arbitrary freedom means the victory of the powerful, which can prevent equal opportunities. Only a freedom which is regulated for the sake of equal freedom is real freedom.

What chances the market has of realizing freedom ultimately depends on the distribution of opportunities of access. When the competition over new products begins – often already at the stage of research and technical innovation – some always have better chances to stake the new 'claims' in the general gold rush (e.g. gene technology). So the arbitrariness of the market should be removed by an overall ordering and its freedom should be developed. But is such an overall ordering universally possible? And if it is not universally possible, is it all the easier to avoid, the more international a business is? Against such a background the reflections of the economist Karl Homann seem naive. He describes the situation as follows: 'The great social innovation of the market economies of the Western world at the beginning of modern times consists in their distinction between two levels in social innovation, the level of the overall ordering and the level of the actions within this overall ordering.'[3]

4. The model of the *social* market economy combines the dynamic of equal freedom in supply and demand with the social dynamic of protecting the weaker and allowing them to participate. Here the social dynamic is predominantly concerned with the protection of goods which are inalienable and at no one's disposal, e.g. health, rights of participation, social rights. However, given the increasing scarcity of resources, the combination of solidarity and freedom which was once praised is now in decline. Here, too, the constitutional society risks losing ground. On the other hand it is clear that we have to find a new balance, because among other things we have been living beyond our resources. But since the weak enjoyed these privileges least, we are least justified in piling the restrictions on them above all.

The principle of social ethics that a measure is to be judged by whether it brings the greatest benefit to those most disadvantaged must continue to be preserved.[4]

The concept of solidarity is often too imprecise and covers many sins because it applies the term solidarity to so many things: compassion, good will, love of neighbour and institutions and laws. The first level, that of individual disposition, is becoming stronger; the second level, that of institutional ties, is declining. There are many individual initiatives which act in solidarity: ecological Third World groups, aid and self-help groups for the socially disadvantaged, the handicapped, foreigners, urban vagrants, drug addicts, those with AIDS and many others. Sometimes they are linked together, but, as the sociologist Karl Gabriel complains, there is no meaningful overall concept.[5] This is also made difficult by the individual option for particular solidarities. Here one can speak of selective solidarity (in accordance with biographical options) and in some circumstances of 'solidarity with the most remote'. It may make sense to set up a children's home in Chile, but in so doing people are possibly overlooking the slums in their own city. Alternatives of this kind should not develop, but rather co-operation. The institutions must get to know the initiatives of individual groups and work with them, and vice versa. Many institutions suffer from fossilization, rigidity and a corresponding loss of credibility. But things cannot be done without them, though sometimes not without their reform.

5. In a situation where solidarity is declining or becoming individualized, another alliance seems to be functioning: that between technology, economics and individual interests (which can be discovered by surveys and thus organized). That can be demonstrated from the progress in biomedicine. The promise of healing a series of illnesses which were previously incurable – e.g. monogene hereditary illnesses, cancer, immune deficiencies and AIDS – is bringing together and encouraging interest groups of the sick, who in turn are exercising pressure for further developments in diagnosis: prenatal diagnosis and gene tests on children, tests on embryos at an early stage, and so on. Sometimes these developments are useful for the so-called pre-implantation diagnosis which is already legally permissible on certain conditions, for example, in France and Sweden. Like the emotional argument, these developments such as the patenting of human genes (and of animals like the cancer mouse whose genes are technically altered) appeal to the argument that they will help seriously ill people. In reality, however this help is still in the very distant future, since so far not even the initial basis for a causal gene therapy has been mastered. A responsible argument would have to begin from the actual technical possibilities and the realistic prospects. But the language of science has become the language of advertising. The commercial list of

means and apparatuses for tests is already a long one. The 'location debate' – i.e. whether Europe can compete with Japan and the USA – is developing social and political pressure, and the noble argument about helping the incurably ill easily skips the questionable nature of the intermediate stages: e.g. the clearly selective methods of early genetic diagnosis. Nowadays supply has many means of strengthening itself in the guise of demand.

6. Therefore today we need an alternative market of 'solidarity'. This market should organize itself on real freedom, on constitutional goods and on ethical principles. It is present when commodities are directly exchanged without any intermediary, in order to support weaker finances and budgets. It is present when people collaborate 'from below' in the service sector, to share jobs and thus provide more employment rather than being under the central planning of employers; it is present when a college sets up an internal crèche in order to help women combine reproduction and a profession; it is present when forces which act anonymously on the market are disclosed and shown up for what they are; it is present when people are not forced out of our society or to the periphery; it is present when people exchange their arguments freely in the face of the dangers that threaten and through shared discussion discover the right way forward.

7. One can observe the marketing of those in need of help in the case of the incurably ill.

At the moment the discussion of a European convention of human dignity and human rights in biomedical research and practice is occupying a key position. One of the most important points under discussion is research which does not benefit them on people who cannot give their consent. In the drafts of this convention on human rights, the conditions of access to such people is made formally difficult, but in fact possibilities of the exploitation of people with the same illness should be regarded in just the same light as possibilities of exploitation of people of the same age or the same state. This is a practice which is increasingly creeping in in compromise negotiations: the wall is a big one, the open door in it is small, but behind it a wealth of possibilities are developing which are no longer being regulated. While the *rules* of the game may have satisfied the spectator, the *moves* in the game can only be limited to a very small degree. Moreover we can doubt whether the integration of human rights in the lands of the great European Community can be secured by so many compromise formulae, which each interprets in a different way. If only the level of minimal consent is in fact affected, then this leads to pressure being put on the member states which have strict regulations to deregulate in the interest of their economic position, i.e. so that they become competitive on the market. The examples of marketing go far beyond this case. When assisted reproduction (*in vitro* fertilization with embryo transfer), despite or because of its low success rate (14–20%), moves on to the 'market' of gene technology in order to lure presumably pestered gene bearers into a method whose help consists in roulette with embryos and the selection of embryos, the policy often sees biotechnology as an economic factor instead of looking at it in constitutional terms. Basic goods which people need for life, like health, the inviolability of the body, dignity independent of ability to achieve – none of this may be endangered if we want to go on living in a humane society in the future.

8. The total market is incompatible with human dignity.

This thesis of Christian anthropology[6] does not overlook the fact that the functions of the market and of competition can be useful instruments. But these functions are only like the social bracket provided by a constitutional society which embraces them. If this bracket is loosened, if it is too weak or does not exist at all, the market develops the strength of the strong and the weakness of the weak; it pulls them apart and polarizes them. Moreover the question arises whether everything that is human and part of life can become a commodity and be exchanged. Human dignity must remain free of the market, and those elements of the environment, freedom and the law which are necessary for life cannot be commercialized. Although this is morally clear, the insight is already being subordinated to commerce, e.g. in the prostitution of human feelings in the media. The confusion of human freedom with the free play of forces usually produces restrictions on freedom.

The Cassandra message of Silvia Strahm-Bernet on the 'free market economy'[7] seems one of a realism which is not at all bitter:

> Asked for visions compatible with humanity they murmur 'market'. Day by day, like a litany. There is no God who can be upset so much as the market, no prayer which is so ardent as the call for market share. 'Economic location' is the altar on which the high priests . . . sacrifice: jobs, social clauses, labour costs. This is called the logic of the market, and it is absolute and transcends all our responsibilities . . . Basically the production of goods is no longer rewarding; it is better to let money work instead of people. The future belongs to the stock exchange, not to the factory . . . It would do us good if in this labyrinth of pressures, market laws and the logic of capital we could speak of guilt . . . It is also strange that trade is allowed many errors, but not those which condemn this trade.

Basically the moral problem of the market is simple: one should not put the second in first place, the market before the bracket which is concerned with the inviolability of the body, human rights, democracy and solidarity, but vice versa. The instrumentalism of the market is all right if it is regulated by the bracket within which it is enclosed. Often the bracket is there, but it does not have the power which the instrument itself develops against it. Thus the policy is no longer master of itself, and becomes all the more remote from its ethical basis.

The total market functions best when it is abstract: with the abstract units of money and currency indexes as commodities. In that way it can be digitalized better and kept free from the masses. People without markets have no future. Markets without people have one. It is not this observation but the situation which is cynical. Anyone who plays an instrument determines when he play it, how he plays it, and with whom or for whom he plays it. A reversal of this situation in the name of the freedom of the instrument would be slavery for the person concerned.

Translated by John Bowden

Notes

1. Cf. D. Mieth, *Schwangerschaftsabbruch. Die Herausforderung und die Alternativen*, Freiburg 1991.

2. At the moment of the writing of this article (September 1996) an EC directive is being discussed in the European Parliament. It includes – on certain conditions – 'patents' on living beings (plants, animals, human biological 'material').

3. Karl Homann, *Moral in den Funktionszusammenhängen der modernen Wirtschaft*, a lecture printed by the Catholic Academy of the diocese of Rottenburg Stuttgart, 13. Homann attempts to bring out this distinction through a distinction in sport between rules of the game and moves in the game. This imagery includes rules, referees and supervisory institutions. These are responsible for the morality of solidarity or for justice: by contrast, in moves in the game or the actions of businesses, the dominant principle is that of competition and efficiency, i.e. the competition which within the framework remains free from the moral assumptions. The competition ensures that the citizens are optimally provided with goods and services. This is because of the pressure of supply.

4. The principle comes from the liberal American social philosopher John Rawls, *A Theory of Justice*, 1971.

5. Cf. *Handeln in der Weltgesellschaft: Christliche Dritte-Welt-Gruppen*, ed. Karl Gabriel et al., Zentralstelle Weltkirche bei der Deutschen Bischofskonferenz, Bonn, December 1995. This notable study by a scholarly working party ends with its own recommendations for collaboration between these groups and the church. It regards the groups as 'building blocks for a society capable of solidarity and empathy' which has 'not yet been discovered and therefore has been criminally neglected by the church authorities' (ibid., 99).

6. Cf. Rudolf Weth (ed.), *Totaler Markt und Menschenwürde. Herausforderungen und Aufgaben christlicher Anthropologie heute*, Neukirchen 1996.

7. In *Neue Wege* 90, 1996, 197–9.

Economics and Ethics in the Development of the Italian Health System

Adriano Bompiani

This article will be chiefly concerned with the Italian experience, but that is in many respects similar to the experience of other advanced industrialized Western countries, above all in Europe.

In Italy, too, the substantial demographic and epidemiological changes which have taken place in the last fifty years (e.g. the overall ageing of the population, the reduction of infectious pathology, the increase in degenerative illnesses), combined with relevant social phenomena (for example voluntary birth control and the progressive increase in the number of women working outside the home), to which can be added the increased capacity to cure acute illness, the constant development of technology and the growing demand for 'the enjoyment of good health' as the right of the individual, have led to the development of new approaches to health systems.

Moreover in Italy, too, the social security system created from the 1950s onwards (on the model of the welfare state), the financial requirements of which have grown much more rapidly than the rate of gross national product and the yield that can be gained from tax revenue, is in crisis.

Finally in Italy, as in other countries of the European community, it is also difficult to pursue a strategy of promoting health based on preventative measures, e.g. the early identification (and neutralization) of the organic, psychological and social factors which can produce pathology, a strategy based not only on the intervention of technology but also on actions involving the community and the development of primary care.

Despite these difficulties, there is no doubt that the development of the right to health care for all the population which has been ratified in Italy, along with increased sensitivity to the so-called 'social rights of citizens', has led to particular ethical importance being attached to this sector. Here the principle of justice is paramount, and in practice is translated into the principle of equity.

It is the relationship between the principle of equity and the economics of health care that I wish to consider here.

The inspiration of solidarity and the concept of equity in health policy

Our country, with the 1948 constitution and above all the 1978 health reform, aims to achieve standards of care which are guaranteed independently of the contract with individual categories or the income of those receiving it.

In 1978 the principle of equal access to the health service for all Italian citizens was approved: this was the affirmation of so-called formal equity.

However, it must be noted that the achievement of levels of substantial equity in meeting health needs is still a long way off.

In 1985 the World Health Organization itself stated that the inequalities in health, again noted widely across European countries, had to be reduced by at least 25% before the end of the century; however, we need to note that within the same country, too, there are factors of inequality which it is necessary and possible to remove.

In Italy, as in other Western states, epidemiological surveys have demonstrated a positive correlation between morbidity/mortality and a low socio-economic level for some pathologies (e.g. cancer) and in exposure to known risk factors (smoking, alcohol, etc.), as well as professional risk factors.

Important correlations with social differences – here including the level of education – are to be found in access to and use of programmes of maternity and child-care instruction; the early diagnosis of women's cancers; recourse to specialist medicine; balanced diets and exposure to other risk factors which are defined as 'preventable' (or 'avoidable'). Possible prevention consists both in the removal of known factors of risk (e.g. inadequate diet, bad housing, working conditions which carry the risk of illness) and the correction of risky life-styles and individual forms of behaviour (smoking, alcohol, drugs), replacing them with life-styles which promote health: physical exercise in leisure time, dental hygiene, road safety, and finally periodical participation in screening for early diagnoses.

These general facts, now well known, must not remain 'sterile' and simply confined to the sphere of knowledge.

At the epidemiological level, in the next few years it will be necessary to study thoroughly surveys of risks for more homogeneous groups of the population in more closely defined areas, and to promote large-scale campaigns of education and information for the population concerned.

Furthermore it will be essential to make social and economic policies concerned to improve the living conditions interact with health policies at the individuals and group level.

No real progress will be made in safeguarding of health unless there is a greater economic commitment on the part of social welfare: the question is particularly urgent among the elderly sector of the population.

Factors of equity in the general organization of health care

It seems useful to emphasize some aspects which the concept of equity offers for a better 'return' from health organization in the years to come.

The aims to be achieved by adopting the concept of equity in the health sector derive from theories of social justice which – as a matter of principle – call for distribution of what is supplied in proportion to need; that also includes the right to equal treatment for equal needs.

The adoption of this concept of 'equity' in health is intuitively subjected to the restraint of available resources; but it is important to investigate the mechanisms by which equity becomes the criterion for also expressing the concept of solidarity.

'Contractualism', now firmly rooted throughout society, today tends to exploit the role of the mere guarantee of the state over against that of the right of citizens to 'paternal protection' in the 1950s, a role which became clearly insufficient in its results and an encumbrance for the bureaucracy which administered it.

It is, then, essential for the state to define the specific guarantees that citizens enjoy (what viable services they get for their rights), going beyond sterile, sweeping and often impracticable theoretical proposals.

Almost fatally, however, this tends to establish the 'minimum' that is due to all, and that inevitably produces discontent, attacks on those making political decisions and hesitations on the part of the latter.

The aspirations of individuals and their freedom of choice in the supply of services, etc., are certainly to be furthered, but in a complex which takes account of the general needs and the balance between the rights and duties of citizens, and that is something that the concept of the 'free market' in health does not succeed in expressing.

There are in fact demands for a shift in the balance of health care in favour of weak social groups or 'poor' Italian regions, demands which are to be put in the context of the right of the individual to equal opportunities of care.

Given these premises, it seems useful in the light of the principles of equity to investigate the problems of getting resources for health care, the distribution of these resources and the methods needed to achieve efficiency and effectiveness in health costs.

The acquisition of resources for health in the European countries and in Italy

More generally, in all the Western countries the problem of equity in the allocation of resources to health is seen in the context of the 'system of social welfare' as a whole, and here variations of need appear to be growing continually.

A bioethical problem which has not yet been resolved is that of identifying parameters that are absolutely valid in establishing a just macro-allocation of resources in the various sectors of national life; however, it is certain that this choice must be made on the basis of an objective and well-tried system of reporting the needs in various areas, of such a kind as to prevent disproportionate allocations and points of disturbance in the economic life of the country, but capable of furthering the gradual and proper achievement of the social objective of substantial equality.

In states where there have been advanced welfare policies, all citizens have to contribute to the expenses of health care according to their means, on the basis of a general principle of solidarity (health is paid for by the healthy and not by the sick).

This demand – which is spread throughout the European countries – translates into three possible ways of financing health systems: (*a*) tax on income; (*b*) compulsory social security contributions to fund the health service; (*c*) a 'ticket' on individual services. Private health schemes – in Europe – are for the most part supplementary.

Here the European countries are characterized by a mix which differs greatly from country to country. At present the Italian 'system' claims around 42% through tax, around 38% through the collection of national insurance and 20% through the 'ticket' (the proportion here exceeds 30% in Portugal).

This 'system' of mix – the fruit of the search for a balance which has gone on for a long time and over which there is political conflict – has so far seemed the most suitable for the Italian situation also; however, some countries have gone for higher levels of taxation (e.g. Sweden, the United Kingdom and Denmark), while others (e.g. France) defend the principle of a greater contribution from social charges.

There are always 'tickets' in the various European countries, to a level never less than 10% of the total income for health care, and despite many reservations they are maintained, because they are a good dissuasive against pharmaceutical waste.

The inter-regional distribution of resources in the case of Italy and the proposal for so-called 'fiscal federalism' in health

We must now consider another problem which – at least in Italy – has become a major one: the claim by various local populations (communities) that they themselves should define the levels of drawing on resources and the quotas to be applied to health.

At present there is a discussion about whether in addition to the general economy of the administration of the National Health Service it would be useful to have a further 'thrust' towards regionalization, through the creation of a federalist health system based on so-called 'fiscal federation'.

The institution of the Inter-Regional Health Fund, which measures needs on the basis of a uniform *per capita* quota for inhabitants in each region – which ensures the immediate transfer by the state – has produced 'equality of opportunity' in health treatment for each citizen, at least at a theoretical level.

However, it has emerged that this results in significant transfers of resources from some of the regions of the north to regions in the south – estimated at 8,300 billion lira a year. In fact the quotas for the needs of the National Health Service at a regional level are 58% in Campania and Calabria, as opposed to 121% in Lombardy and 113% in Piedmont.

That has caused resentments in the northern regions, which are also expressed at the political level.

Hence the proposal that each region procures for itself the resources that it wants to go to health.

The question is a controversial one in terms of equity; in any case, even if the current criterion for creating the fund is made permanent, it has to be remembered that distribution in accordance with a uniform *per capita* quota does not correspond to the principles of substantial equity if one takes into account the different demographic context of the regions.

There is a need to correct the allocation by weighted quotas, which take into account the characteristics of the resident population.

The commitment of health resources and economic rationalization of costs

It is above all against costs that polemic is directed in the debate on the future of health care in the various European countries.

Since these costs are judged excessive everywhere, in recent years not only have provisions to reduce the allocations been adopted, but there have also been more or less successful attempts to reduce expenses by quantifying them at the level of individual 'acts of care'.

At all events, here it should be noted that in a table of health costs in the various European countries, Italy is in the high median range (around 8.5% of GIP). Further reductions in the allocations to health do not seem to me possible; on the other hand, every effort must be made to improve the return on resources. In other words, it is important to spend better. This is a widespread view among economists, among the more well-informed doctors and in public opinion.

It also leads us to consider, briefly, two criteria which should secure a better commitment of resources: the market-programme equation and the 'commercialization' of the larger health structures.

The market/programme equation

As already in other countries, from 1 January 1995 a system has been implemented in Italy which is to lead to the introduction of the so-called programmed internal market in the sense of the supply of care by various health structures but at prices fixed (reimbursed) by the state.

This criterion does not correspond to the 'market' in the technical sense as defined by economists since it lacks the prime and indispensable requisite for a situation of true competition: a plurality of producers and consumers. The vast majority of hospital bodies (producers of services) belong to the same firm as the consumers (the local health authorities).

The experiment is under way, but the course of the first year shows that the tariffs fixed for reimbursements do not always cover the costs, and this penalizes particularly the services of specialist scientific treatment and care and some sectors of specialized treatment (e.g. paediatrics) in university polyclinics and institutes. The economic profile of these bodies also differs from that of the hospitals run by the local health authorities. This makes urgent and drastic corrective measures necessary.

It should also be noted that while the process of the 'commercialization' of health structures (major hospitals, university polyclinics offering specialized treatment and the local health authorities) is being pursued, it should not be mythicized, attributing immediate effects and exceptional efficacy to it.

The principle of commercialization is not one that is easy to understand and must mature in the awareness not only of the operators (doctors and nurses in particular) but also of the administrators.

Bioethical questions and economic aspects of individual acts of care and therapy

We have examined problems which can be defined as the macro-allocation of resources, in respect both of the 'health budget' and the distribution of its resources among major territorial units (regions).

However, it is also necessary to consider the questions which arise – at an economic level – beyond this dimension, since it is well known that health costs are determined by a myriad actions which are economically more or less relevant, performed at the level of the doctor-patient relationship. It is therefore necessary to analyse the process of the micro-allocation of resources at the level of clinical decision, and this leads to a discussion of which of the various patients has the right to receive care and specific treatments, and to what degree.

As is clear, this approach leads to discrimination, which beyond a certain level can no longer be related to the principle of equity and becomes unjust.

At the doctrinal level, this problem, which dominates current bio-ethical reflections, is discussed in terms of utilitarian, individualistic libertarian, egalitarian and finally personalistic orientations.

Social utilitarianism puts forward as an ethical criterion for the allocation of resources cost/benefit analysis, aimed at collective utility. In other words, the costs that society incurs in the area of health should be commensurate to the benefits to be realized, relating to the society as a whole and not to the individual. The aim is the maximizing of the well-being of the greatest possible number of individuals.

It is evident that in its most extreme expressions, utilitarianism risks on the one hand sacrificing the benefit of some individuals for social utility and on the other emphasizing productivity in the quality of life. This leads to the proposal that investments should be eliminated in the care of 'unproductive' patients, those who cannot recover to become the labour force and who are therefore useless (e.g. terminal cancer patients, those with brain damage).

The individualistic libertarian theory, following Noziik's view, puts the accent on justice, interpreting it as a recognition of the rights and freedom of the individual. In the distribution of health resources this perspective applies the free market rule: it emphasizes the 'capacity to pay', along with social utility and public interest. The role of the state in this context is minimal: the state limits itself to guaranteeing the rights and freedoms of the individual.

It is evident that by emphasizing the autonomy of the individual, individualism risks losing sight of the common good and the role of the state.

The egalitarian theory argues that the distribution of health care must be equal for all. Any deviation from absolute equality of distribution is unjust, and the scarcity of resources does not justify differences in distribution.

In seeking to guarantee to all a minimum of care, of quality and quantity of life, egalitarianism does not consider the particular requirements of the person in the social context when services above the minimum are required.

Finally, personalistic bioethics – putting the prime value of the person at the centre of its reflection – proposes a co-ordination of means and resources and a health programme based on the principle of sociality and subsidiarity.

In this case the criteria to be applied to the selection of priorities among patients are urgency, proportionality in treatment and random selection.

Medical urgency is the prime basic criterion for medical and surgical treatment.

The second is 'therapeutic proportionality', in which the sacrosanct principle of the use of scientifically effective treatments according to 'guidelines' or protocols validated by experience reappears.

The parameter of priorities on waiting lists (or random selection) is considered when the cases of a number of patients are equally urgent.

We should note that though the line of 'personalist bioethics' is the one which gives most support to the tradition of medical ethics, it too requires an interpretation of 'economic parameters' case by case and puts a heavy responsibility on every health operator in using communal resources.

It is in the development of the concept of 'therapeutic proportionality', avoiding giving excessive care on the one hand and inadequate nursing on the other, to be pursued in the years to come, that there should be a strong commitment to educate both health workers and patients.

Conclusions

The above remarks are by no means an 'exhaustive' analysis of the complex series of relations between the right to have health safeguarded and substantial equity in the enjoyment of the health service.

The need to go more deeply into this subject is evident, and in fact there are passionate discussions on it in all industrialized countries.

This is a chapter in that 'social ethics' which has come to the fore so powerfully in recent times. The debate, which is 'bioethical' (given its relevance in terms of its impact on health), already provides an occasion, and will do so even more in Italy in the immediate future, for checking just how far the principle of solidarity posited on the basis of our constitution and that of many European countries, is maturing in popular consciousness.

Translated by John Bowden

Justice, Gender and the Market

Lisa Sowle Cahill

Since the organization of economic relations according to the market can have both just and unjust consequences, the market has received both qualified acceptance and strong criticism in Roman Catholic social teaching.[1] Similarly, the modern market has ambivalent significance for the situations of women, and varies significantly world-wide.

The market can increase the marginality of low-status groups, and offer dominant groups new occasions of self-assertion. The global transfer of capital, through transnational corporations, the International Monetary Fund, and the World Bank, most often serves the interests of 'First World' nations. 'Third World' debtor nations spend more to pay off interest on international loans than on basic social services for their citizens, casting the poor into ever greater economic insecurity and suffering. The vulnerability of women is magnified additionally when an expanding, global, market economy disrupts traditional patterns of life in which individuals had access to material and social goods on the basis of clearly defined social roles in family and local community. Moreover, women are the primary source of cheap labour for national and international manufacturing and industry, especially women in countries where the economy as a whole is precarious. And even in Asia, where Japan, Thailand, Taiwan, Hong Kong, South Korea and Singapore enjoy rising market competitiveness, low-paid female workers make it possible. Many Asian and Latin American women who provide domestic services or labour in factories are in fact exploited by other women, whose ability to benefit from the low-paid work of others is protected by the high economic status of their own nation or class.[2]

Because of its actual exploitative effects, the market is justly criticized by those who seek a radical restructuring of the global economy, often calling for a new form of socialism in which the participation of formerly excluded groups will contribute to the formation of more inclusive economic structures. However, strikingly, some of the same emerging cultural values, like equality and self-determination, that make the market possible have also contributed to women's consciousness of their own oppression and helped to further calls for gender equality. Moreover, increased control over economic activity by individual women and women's collectives continues to be a major agent of gender equalization world-wide. Thus it is difficult to pronounce that the market is either inherently just or unjust. What are clearly unjust are economic relationships which deprive some of the world's population of the basic conditions of a decent life, while enriching others at highly disproportionate rates. Unfortunately, the market, as a present global reality, does just that.

The market refers most simply to 'that series of social patterns of interaction between people who have something that others want and those who are willing to pay in order to get it'. When owners seek the best offer for their product or service, and buyers seek the lowest priced source, market competition tends to control prices without the need of any extensive administrative bureaucracy.[3] This is what makes market relations so attractive a form of social organization for the liberal champions of moral agency as autonomous choice.

Yet marketing in the sense of trading goods and services has undoubtedly been around since the earliest human beings discerned that their neighbours were in possession of something for which they themselves had a keen desire or need. Market as trade has had, historically, tremendous implications for gender relationships, for differential treatment and social agency of men and women, and thus for justice conceived in terms of the essential equality and dignity of all human persons. For one thing, societies have always differed considerably in the degree to which women carry on independent economic activity and retain control over the results of their labours. In *The Creation of Patriarchy*, Gerda Lerner hypothesizes that patriarchy itself may have arisen in a form of trade of women among kin groups who sought exogamous marriages:[4] the 'marketing' of women and their reproductive services, with both 'owners' and 'buyers' defined as a male elder or an extended family unit dominated by male authority. In many or even most of the world's cultures, the marketing of women among kin groups has been the basis for the formation of marriages and the extenuation of the family descent line, property holdings and social power through advantageous alliances. Thus, to the extent that traditional economies were structured by market values, women have themselves been treated as marketable commodities, and have understood their own access to material goods in terms of the market value of their sexual and reproductive capacities, whether as wives, mothers, concubines or prostitutes. Even where women have gained freedom to consent to marriages, they have typically continued to trade their youth and fertility for male protection, both social and economic.

But the market as we know it in the twentieth century operates under some characteristically modern assumptions about human agency and relationships. Beginning in the sixteenth century in Europe, both the cultural consciousness and the structural reality of economic relations went through some important transitions. Historically, the Enlightenment signalled a new confidence in human reason and in the power of human freedom to cast off traditional ways of doing things and initiate change in what had previously seemed the irresistible laws of nature or orderings of divine creation. At the same time, increased communication among continents and cultures, especially voyages between Europe and the Americas, encouraged the emergence of a 'global' consciousness and a sense that individuals and groups of investors, not only kings and emperors, could exercise their agency on a world scale, and could compete for economic control of faraway lands and their resources.

From the sixteenth to the nineteenth centuries, Europe and North America witnessed an amazing series of new inventions, stemming partly from the new mind-set in which the human condition seems open, subject to human intervention, and capable of reorganization into new patterns unlike those people had accepted for centuries. 'Rather than taking the current situation for granted, they began to assume that things could be improved – whether through science and engineering, through national political change, or through discussion and decision in a small local 'organization'.[5]

In the twentieth century, especially after the Second World War, we have also seen the emergence of the United Nations and a global concept of human rights. This concept is often disputed in terms of both its specific content and its Western, liberal bias. Yet it is one mechanism for heightening the modern consciousness of basic human equality and bringing repressive or discriminatory social practices to the light of international scrutiny. The perception that human beings are free and equal individuals, able to determine their own choices and be responsible for their own destinies, is also an important part of the mentality of the modern market.

Another factor in the modern period is the emergence of the economy as a sphere of activity that is relatively independent of other institutions such as religion, family and politics. Prestige and influence in one of these spheres is often in fact translated, legitimately or illegitimately, into the power to exert one's will and agency in another. Yet modern cultures understand the economy to be an essentially distinct institution. Access to money is not necessarily connected with status in other spheres, and not all goods in other spheres should be traded for money. Indeed, criticisms of the modern market grow loudest when it is intertwined with other spheres of value, through the 'commodification' of goods like sex, reproduction, health care and scientific knowledge.[6]

The market, then, is possible precisely because of the rise of the modern individual – as free, equal, and possessing transformative social agency. 'Market' in the modern sense also depends on the realization that the effects of individual agency can be global in scope – can be exercised in a realm of communication or participation that extends far beyond the local village, nearest town, or even national boundaries. On the one hand, these dimensions of contemporary economic life license social change and personal self-determination, including women's independence. On the other, they have led to exaggerations and abuses. The perniciousness of market values lies in their amenability to the same forces of domination which often defined status in traditional, hierarchical societies, and which can even pervert socialist cooperation. Just as a social system in which women, slaves, certain ethnic or racial groups, or certain castes are devalued operates on a principle of dehumanization of some of the members of the system, so market societies can dehumanize some members and systematically deprive them of access to socio-economic agency.

To the extent that the modern 'market society' is global in reach, it also permits an international and inter-cultural form of dehumanization, in which entire peoples or classes of people are excluded from the economic community in which productive work is compensated by the material and social goods which support full participation in the common good. One has only to look at the world-wide patterns of colonialism which were perpetrated in the wake of the Enlightenment to see that its emancipation of 'man' hardly ended the human proclivity to include some and exclude others from the circle of what we consider full human and personal value. As refracted through the market, this same tendency is manifested in self-centred individualism: the reduction of human rationality to 'instrumental reason' focussed only on the most efficient means to economic profit; the working assumption that every human good has an exchange value on the market, and can be bought or sold ('commodification'); and the impersonality and amoralism of market forces, according to which the redistribution of goods depends on competition ('efficiency'), and in which competition depends solely on the individual preferences of buyers and sellers who already have the means and opportunity to enter the market ('market value'). Human values that remain outside the market with its norms of productivity and profit – such as the human dignity of the young, elderly or poor, and our duty to future generations – become quickly marginalized in the institutions and practices of the society governed by the market.[7]

Moreover, the assumption that social relations will be governed by market demand is linked to the idea that individual competitors work on subjective preference alone. This readily produces an atmosphere of moral relativism, with individual choice as the only absolute. A relativisitic norm of market efficiency discourages evaluation of the objective morality of the aims of the market and its human agents. It deflects inspection of the justice of the human relations the market produces. In this way, an economic system which began with the exaltation of human freedom, reason, equality and agency ends with the degradation of the humanity of those who are excluded from competition by the same forces of domination and violence which institutionalized inequality in more 'traditional' societies. Moreover, the local communities in which individuals were once able to define their roles in relation to the social good, to receive some measure of security in respect of such roles, and to exercise some measure of control over their own future and that of their children, are being destroyed. Market forces subordinate family and other local networks to economic productivity and profit as conceived on an ever larger, transnational scale.

In what way do these phenomena bear on the question of women's roles and status in a market society? First of all, feminist criticisms of social relations have been inspired in large part by the same shifts in human consciousness that made the market possible. And some feminist aims are similar to those of the market. For example, the call for recognition of women's full humanity and social participation has drawn strength from Enlightenment ideals of freedom, self-determination and equality, as well as the basic premise that our history does not absolutely determine our future. The oppressive hierarchies of traditional, closed societies, particularly patriarchy, have been challenged primarily in those same cultures in which a market economy is now prevalant. The recognition that reproductive and domestic work has social value equal to the 'productive' work or 'wage labour' has no doubt been furthered by the tendency of the market mentality to look at everything in terms of cost, benefit and exchange value. Women are no longer to be treated as the virtual property of men, but are to be in control of their own productive and reproductive capacities. Women's education and economic activity are also recognized as the keys to their social independence from male control, and as the prerequisites of women's positive contributions to the many dimensions of a healty common life. Yet it is important to recognize that as women gain more socio-economic power in some sectors of society or nations, they often continue to exploit other women whose labour helps make their lifestyle possible.

During the 1995 United Nations Fourth World Conference on Women in Beijing, the world's attention was drawn to the need for and effectiveness of self-help projects in which poor women used very little resources – a small loan, a few tools, some goats or bee-hives – to take major steps toward economic independence and an improved way of life. Nancy Barry, president of Women's World Banking, a non-profit institution with affiliates in forty developing countries, believes, 'Women don't need charity, they need access' to the market through personal networks tailored to local opportunities. Bangladesh's Grameen Bank, a model for small-scale credit, lent women $400 million in 1994, including loans as small as one US dollar, and 97% of them were repaid.[8]

However, the market can also become another and more efficient means to exploit women, to the extent that patriarchal hierarchies are not genuinely overcome, and women lack access to market initiatives. When women's nature and roles are defined in terms of sexuality, reproduction and domesticity, and when these 'female' roles are simply overlaid with a market ethos of commodification, moral relativism and the dominance of those who already possess resources and the social opportunity to market them, women's situation degenerates further. Women are not seen as productive or competitive, and are therefore not considered to be entitled to a full share in or control over available social resources.

Albina Peczon Fernandez illustrates this side of the market with the story of a Filipina woman she calls 'María Dolores'.[9] After World War II, the United Nations, under the aegis of the United States and President Harry S. Truman, announced a programme of 'development' for 'Third World' countries. Prior to this venture of making 'scientific progress', technology and industrialization available to underdeveloped areas, María Dolores used her own resources to grow vegetables, raise chickens, clothe her family and find herbal cures for illness. Her husband likewise employed traditional means of farming, and María Dolores put in an equal number of hours planting, weeding, fertilizing and harvesting the crops.

After development began, María Dolores and her family were pushed farther down the scale by schemes from the North which maintained the south in a state of dependency. Many lost their land to the global market, and experienced no positive change in their standards of living. Moreover, only the husband is considered a farmer. María Dolores's work is devalued because it has no exchange value. 'Poor María Dolores! She is already wrinkled and her knowledge regarding the production and reproduction of life meets no demand in the job market. What employers are seeking are single women with education, young in years, good-looking and fluent speakers of English.'[10] Now María Dolores's children and grandchildren are out of work. Only two granddaughters have managed to find work overseas. 'One is a domestic helper in Kuwait. Whenever talk would dwell on the abuse and rape of women in the Arab world, the old woman played deaf. Another is in Japan. Whenever the old woman hears the words "Japayuki" and AIDS, she just allows herself to sink into silence.'[11]

Before the war, this woman may have lived in a patriarchal culture, her labour not rewarded at the same level as a man's, and premature death, especially infant mortality, may have been more frequent than after modernization. But the industrialization of her country and the erosion of traditional ways of life did not improve her status overall, nor that of the women in the next generations. They simply became subject to international market forces which allowed entrepreneurs from prosperous regions to displace them from their customary means of livelihood. Women, meanwhile, were forced to market their bodies and their labour outside the local community where at least some basic protections and entitlements had existed.

Anchalee Singhanetra-Renard shows that a similar situation obtains even in a country like Thailand, in which overt colonization by foreign powers has been avoided, and industrialization has been the project of the indigenous government itself. Moreover, Thai women traditionally shared economic activity with men, especially trading, and enjoyed relatively high status by virtue of matrilineal spirit devotions, entailing the residence of a young couple in the wife's family compound. Yet, although women maintain important religious practices, young girls (from mid-teens to early twenties) are expected to repay their parents' care by contributing to the support and education of younger siblings, especially boys, and helping to purchase land or other commodities. Compared to boys, for whom temporary monastic life made education possible, girls, especially those from poor families, have had relatively less access to education. Thus, when economic opportunities for girls become scarce in the rural communities, they travel to the urban areas, but are not prepared for the better-paying types of skilled labour brought by the growing market economy. Many become sex workers, a fate more readily accepted by them and their families in the light of the traditional expectation that girls have a duty to contribute to the support of the family. Sometimes, with the advent of Western-style goods and luxuries available on the market, the aim of accumulating comforts and status symbols undermines traditional values to the extent that the consignment of a daughter to a brothel is paid as their price. Tourism, including sex tourism, is Thailand's biggest business.[12]

Meanwhile, women in countries with advanced capitalist economies also know that women's traditional association with reproductive and domestic roles, as well as the expectation that women will trade sexual services for their livelihood or for male protection, still survive in cultures where women's rights to education and to equal pay for equal work are theoretically protected by law. 'Women become economically vulnerable through childbearing and child rearing, and employers treat all women differently than all men, as a pattern, because women could be mothers.'[13] Divorce in modern, Western cultures today is so problematic and disadvantageous for women precisely because of the right of men to divorce with little or no continuing economic responsibility for former wives and their children. This represents a repudiation of the economic bargain on which the marriage and the acquisition by the man of the women's domestic and reproductive services depended in the first place.[14] The only real solution, of course, is not to enforce the bargain by law, but to remove from women the necessity of making it, by supporting women's own socio-economic agency. If capitalist cultures are to organize the economy with some measure of justice, they must balance familial and economic roles for both sexes by going beyond sheer market values. Just economic relations cannot be accomplished without parental leaves, child care and elderly care, universal access to health care and education, and legal deterrents to violence in the home and sexual harrassment in the workplace.

It is probably impossible to make a universal assessment of the implications of the market for gender. We may at least note that all modes of accumulating and exercising power are in their own ways prone to corruption, and that women have had less access to power than men in virtually all cultures. Market dynamics certainly have the potential to exacerbate gender inequity, just as they can and have heightened disparities of wealth among peoples and nations. The key to just social institutionalization of the market is the subordination of individual profit to all the many conditions of social life which make up the common good, and to the participation of all members of society in the common good.

A first challenge is to define the common good locally, in relation to the concrete communities of life in which human persons actually flourish. A second and even more difficult task is to locate the local economy positively within the much broader economic networks that link and influence smaller communities world-wide. Not all determinations of the market can be local, due precisely to the fact that injustice often is the direct result of competition for resources and profit on a broader scale. The same 'principle of subsidiarity'[15] which affirms the rightful independence of local bodies and groups also implies that, when the global market creates or exaggerates inequities, wider organization and authority will also be necessary to redistribute resources from locale to locale. Control of the market in today's global arena is notoriously difficult. Nations tend to act in their own economic self-interest, with little sustained consideration of their long-range ethical responsibilites to other peoples or to the world's natural environment. Furthermore, decision-making does not always take place at the level of national governments, or even the IMF, but in corporate boardrooms outside the political process and insulated from public scrutiny. As with armed violence and human-rights violations within and among nations, so with economic injustices: the existence of an international body that could authoritatively define responsibilities and resolve conflicts is still an ideal rather than a reality.

Market relations which promote gender justice can begin with local decision-making by women about the form and extent of their market activity, in line with their own experiences and needs. Sometimes national or international bodies must act to protect women's interests. But the beginning point for gender equality in economic relations is the creation of 'grass-roots' channels for women to voice their needs and concerns, express solidarity with one another, and discover practical, step-by-step ways to increase women's economic power in a context of mutual responsibility.

Notes

1. See David Hollenbach, 'The Market and Catholic Social Teaching', in this issue. I want to thank both David Hollenbach and Kwok, Pui-lan (Episcopal Divinity School, Cambridge, Massachusetts, USA) for offering many helpful comments on this article.

2. See Kwok, Pui-lan, 'Business Ethics in the Economic Development of Asia: A Feminist Analysis', *Asia Journal of Theology* 9/1, 1995, 133–45.

3. Prentiss L. Pemberton and Daniel Rush Finn, *Toward a Christian Economic Ethic: Stewardship and Social Power*, Minneapolis 1985, 125.

4. Gerda Lerner, *The Creation of Patriarchy*, New York 1986.

5. Pemberton and Finn, *Toward a Christian Economic Ethic* (n. 3), 2.

6. See Alan Wolfe, *Whose Keeper? Social Science and Moral Obligation*, Berkeley, Los Angeles and London 1989; Michael Walzer, *Spheres of Justice: A Defense of Pluralism and Equality*, New York 1983.

7. Pemberton and Finn, *Toward a Christian Economic Ethic* (n. 3) 131.

8. Barbara Crossette, 'The Second Sex in the Third World', *The New York Times*, 9 September 1995, E5.

9. Albina Peczon Fernandez, 'The Filipina, Environment and Development', *Lila: Asia-Pacific Women's Studies Journal* 4, 1994, 43–57.

10. Ibid., 47.

11. Ibid., 49.

12. Anchalee Singhanetra-Renard, 'The Complex Relationship Between Production and Reproduction: Ancestor Spirit Cults and Reproductive Choice in the Context of Changing Socio-Economic Conditions in Northern Thailand', *Lila: Asia-Pacific Women's Studies Journal* 4, 1994 , 1–16; Anchalee Singhanetra-Renard and Nitaya Prabhudhanitisarn, 'Changing Socio-Economic Roles of Thai Women and Their Migration', in Sylvia Chant (ed.), *Gender and Migration in Developing Countries*, London and New York 1992, 154–73. See also Sylvia Chant, 'Conclusion: Towards a

Framework for the Analysis of Gender-Selective Migration', in Chant, 197–206. On feminist theology and prostitution in Asia, see Kwok, Pui-lan, 'The Future of Feminist Theology', in Ursula King (ed.), *Feminist Theology from the Third World: A Reader*, Maryknoll, NY 1994, 72–15; and 'Business Ethics' (n. 2), 142–3. In the latter article, Kwok notes the connection between the sex trade and militarism, for prostitution of Asian women to Western men became big business during the Vietnam war, with the arrival of military personnel looking for 'rest and recreation'.

13. Carol S. Robb, *Equal Value: An Ethical Approach to Economics and Sex*, Boston 1995, 23.

14. See Mary Ann Glendon, *Abortion and Divorce in Western Law: American Failures, European Challenges*, Cambridge and London 1987; Susan Moller Okin, *Justice, Gender and the Family*, New York 1989.

15. This principle from Roman Catholic social teaching is discussed in the article by David Hollenbach in this issue. It was initially presented by Leo XIII, against Marxist socialism, as requiring the legitimate independence of social groups from state control. However, in view of the emerging post-war international community, John XXIII reinterpreted it to require also the legitimate intervention of the state or national government, or even of the world government, in situations of injustice.

Contributors

FRANCISCO GÓMEZ CAMACHO, SJ, holds doctorates in theology and economic sciences. He lectures in Economic History at the Pontifical University in Madrid and in the History of Economic Thought at the University of Salamanca. He specializes in the study of economic thought in Spanish scholasticism of the sixteenth and seventeenth centuries and has published translations from the Latin, with introductions, of four classic texts. He has also contributed 'Spanish Economic Thought in the Seventeenth Century' to *Economic Effects of the European Expansion*, edited by J. Casas Pardo (1992).

Address: Universidad Pontificia Comillas, Alberto Aguileraze, 28015, Madrid, Spain.

BRUNO KERN was born in Vienna in 1958 and studied theology and philosophy there, in Fribourg and in Munich, gaining a doctorate in theology. After working as an academic assistant with the Franciscans in Bonn between 1985 and 1990, he became Lektor in theology for Matthias Grünewald Verlag in Mainz and editor of the German language edition of *Concilium*. As chair of the ecology commission of Pax Christi he is now primarily concerned with the relationship of ecology to economy. Among his many relevant publications are *Theologie im Horizont des Marxismus. Zur Geschichte der Marxismusrezeption in der lateinamerikanischen Theologie der Befreiung*, Mainz 1992, and (with Leonard Boff), *Werkbuch Theologie der Befreiung. Anliegen – Streitpunkte – Personen. Materialien and Texte*, Düsseldorf 1988.

Address: Münsterstrasse 10/64, 551166 Mainz, Germany.

BEATRIZ MELANO COUCH was born and educated in Argentina, and after studying at the University of Buenos Aires and Princeton Theological Seminary received her doctorate in theology from the University of Strasbourg. She has been a guest professor in San Franciso, Denver, Colorado and Bangalore and has lectured widely for the Methodist Church in England, The Canadian Forum of Churches of Canada, and in most countries of Latin America, as well as in the USA and Europe. For many years she has been a professor at the Theological Ecumenical Seminary in Buenos Aires. She has written many articles and two books, *La mujer y la iglesia*, the first book to appear on the subject in Latin America, and *Hermenéutica metódica*.

Address: Francisco Bilbao 1645, 1406 Buenos Aires, Argentina.

GREGORY BAUM was born in Berlin in 1923; since 1940 he has lived in Canada. He studied at McMaster University in Hamilton, Ontario; Ohio State University; the University of Fribourg, Switzerland; and the new School for Social Research in New York. He is Master of Arts and Doctor of Theology and is now Professor Emeritus at the Faculty of Religious Studies of McGill University, Montreal. He is editor of *The Ecumenist*. His publications include *Religion and Alienation* (1975); *The Priority of Labor* (1982); *Essays in Critical Theology* (1992); and *Karl Polanyi on Ethics and Economics* (1996).

Address: McGill University, 3520 University Street, Montreal, PO, H3A 2A7, Canada.

ULRICH DUCHROW is Professor of Systematic Theology in the University of Heidelberg. His writings include *Global Economy: A Confessional Issue for the Churches*, Geneva 1987; *Shalom – Biblical Perspectives on Creation, Justice and Peace*, Geneva 1989; *Total War Against the Poor: Confidential Documents of the 17th Conference of American Armies*, New York 1990; *Europe in the World System 1492–1992: Is Justice Possible?*, Geneva 1992; and *Alternatives to Global Capitalism: Drawn from Biblical History, Designed for Political Action*, Utrecht 1995.

Address: Hegenichstrasse 22, 19124 Heidelberg, Germany.

FRANÇOIS HOUTART was born in 1925, ordained priest in 1949, and gained his doctorate in sociology at the Catholic University of Louvain, of which he is professor emeritus. At present he is Director of the Tricontinental Centre at Louvain-la-Neuve and is editor of two journals, *Social Compass* and *Alternatives Sud*. He has written around fifty works on the sociology of religion, development and culture, and many articles on the same topics.

Address: Centre Tricontinental, Avenue Sainte Gertrude 5, B 1348 Ottignies-Louvain-la-Neuve, Belgium.

BERNARD TEO was born in Singapore in 1952. After joining the Redemptorists in 1971 he studied first in Singapore and then in India before being ordained priest in 1979. He then spent five years working as a missionary in Singapore and Malaysia, including a year lecturing in theology at the Penang seminary. In 1985 he went to the Catholic University of America, where he received his doctorate in moral theology in 1989. Since 1991 he has taught fundamental moral theology and ethics on the theology faculty of the Yarra Theological Union in Melbourne, Australia.

Address: 15–19 Sweetland Road, Box Hill, Victoria 3128, Australia.

DAVID HOLLENBACH SJ is the Margaret O'Brien Flatley Professor of Catholic Theology at Boston College. He has recently served as visiting professor at Hekima College, Nairobi, Kenya. His publications include *Catholicism and Liberalism: Contributions to American Public Philosophy*, edited with R. Bruce Douglass, Cambridge 1994; *Justice, Peace, and Human Rights: American Catholic Social Ethics in a Pluralistic World*, New York 1988; *Claims in Conflict: Retrieving and Renewing the Catholic Human Rights Tradition*, New York 1979. He is past president of the Society of Christian Ethics, USA (1995–1996). He assisted the US Bishops in drafting their 1986 pastoral letter *Economic Justice for All: Catholic Social Teaching and the US Economy*.

Address: Boston College, Department of Theology, 404 Carney Hall, Chestnut Hill, Massachusetts 02167–3806, USA.

ANTONIO LATTUADA was born in 1945 and was ordained priest in the diocese of Milan in 1969, after studying at the Pontifical Gregorian University. He is currently teaching moral theology at the Catholic University of the Sacred Heart in Milan and the Theological Faculty of Southern Italy. He has written *Etica normativa*, Milan 1985, and has had articles published in collections, including *Introduzione all bioetica*, Milan 1986; *Educare all'uso responsabile del danaro*, Rome 1996; *Diritti umani*, Casale Monferrato 1995.

Address: Via F. Carcano 18, 21047 Saronno, Italy.

ENRIQUE DUSSEL was born in Argentina in 1934. With a degree in theology and a doctorate in philosophy, he lectures on ethics and church history in Mexico. He is president of the study commission on church history of Latin America, and a founder member of the Ecumenical Association of Third World Theologians. He is the author of numerous works on

theology and the history of the church in Latin America, among which the
following have recently appeared in English: *Ethics and the Theology of
Liberation* (1978); *History of the Church in Latin America, 1492–1980*
(1981); *Papers for Liberataion Theology* (1981).

MARCIANO VIDAL, C.Ss.R., was born in 1937 in the León region of Spain.
A Redemptorist priest, he holds a degree in theology from the Pontifical
University of Salamanca, and a doctorate in moral theology from the
Alfonsiana in Rome. He teaches moral theology at the Comillas Pontifical
University of Madrid, where he is director of the Higher Institute of Moral
Sciences. He is a member of the editorial board of *Concilium*. His major
published works are: *Moral de Actitudes* (4 vols., 1990–91, now in its
eighth edition); *Diccionario de Etica teológico* (1991); *Frente al rigorismo
moral, la benignidad pastoral* (1986); *La propuesta moral de Juan Pablo II*
(1994), most of which have been translated into Italian and Portuguese;
and, most recently, *La familia en la vida y en la obra de Alfonso de Liguori
(1696–1787)* (1995).

Address: Manuel Silvela 14, 28010 Madrid, Spain.

IRING FETSCHER was born in Marbach/Neckar in 1922 and studied in
Tübingen and Paris. From 1963 to 1988 he was Professor of Political
Science and Social Philosophy in Frankfurt. His *Karl Marx and Marxism*
appeared in English (1967); other important publications are *Rousseaus
politische Philosophie* (1970) and *Überlebensbedingungen der Menschheit*,
Berlin 1991.

Address: Ganghoferstrasse 20, 60320 Frankfurt am Main, Germany.

DIETMAR MIETH was born in 1940 and studied theology, German and
philosophy. He gained his doctorate in theology at Würzburg in 1968 and
his Habilitation in theological ethics in Tübingen in 1974. He became
Professor of Moral Theology in Fribourg, Switzerland in 1974 and
Professor of Theological Ethics in Tübingen in 1981. His publications
include *Die Einheit von vita activa und vita contemplativa*, Regensburg
1969; *Dichtung, Glaube und Moral*, Mainz 1976; *Epik und Ethik*,
Tübingen 1976; *Moral und Erfahrung*, Fribourg CH ³1983; *Meister
Eckhart* (which he edited), Munich ³1986; *Gotteserfahrung – Weltverant-
wortung*, Munich 1982; *Die neue Tugenden*, Düsseldorf 1984; *Ehe als
Entwurf*, Mainz 1984; *Arbeit und Menschenwürde*, Freiburg im Breisgau

1985; *Die Spannungseinheit von Theorie und Praxis*, Fribourg CH and Freiburg im Breisgau 1986.

Address: Blumenstrasse 3, D7401 Neustetten I, Germany.

LISA SOWLE CAHILL is Associate Professor of Christian Ethics at Boston College. She received her doctorate in theology from the University of Chicago Divinity School in 1976, after completing a dissertation entitled *Euthanasia: A Protestant and a Catholic Perspective*. Recent research interests include method in theological ethics, the use of scripture in ethics, medical ethics, and sexual ethics. Articles on these subjects have appeared in American journals such as *Theological Studies, Journal of Religious Ethics, Journal of Medicine and Philosophy, Chicago Studies, Religious Studies Review, Interpretation, Horizons*, and *The Linacre Quarterly*. She has also written *Between the Sexes: Toward a Christian Ethics of Sexuality*. She also serves as an Associate Editor of *Journal of Religious Ethics, Religious Studies Review*, and *Horizons*.

Address: Boston College, Dept. of Theology, Chestnut Hill, Mass. 02167–3806, USA.

The editors wish to thank the great number of colleagues from the various Advisory Committees who contributed in a most helpful way to the final project.

W. Beuken	Louvain	Belgium
B. Melano Couch	Buenos Aires	Argentina
K. Demmer	Rome	Italy
E. Dussel	Mexico City	Mexico
T. Goffi	Brescia	Italy
F. Houtart	Louvain-la-Neuve	Belgium
B. van Iersel	Nijmegen	The Netherlands
F. Menne	Münster	Germany
H. Oppenheimer	Jersey	Channel Islands
E. Pace	Padua	Italy
P. Röttlander	Aachen	Germany

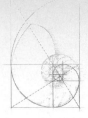

JOHN TEMPLETON FOUNDATION

announces the

1997 CALL FOR EXEMPLARY PAPERS

in

HUMILITY THEOLOGY

To encourage scholarly research on matters of both spiritual and scientific significance, the John Templeton Foundation invites scholars to submit papers on topics regarding the constructive interaction of:

- Theology and the natural sciences
- Religion and the medical sciences, or
- Religion and the human behavioral sciences.

These papers must proceed from professional scholarship and display a spirit of intellectual humility, a respect for varied theological traditions, and an attitude of open-minded inquiry into the varied ways in which theology/religion and the empirical sciences can be mutually informative.

Prizes of $2,000 will be awarded in November 1997. The deadline for submission of papers is June 1, 1997. (Please designate one of the three broad subject areas when submitting a paper.)

To be eligible for award consideration, a paper must also:

- Have been accepted for publication or published since June 1994, in a peer-reviewed scholarly journal, or in some other comparably selective scholarly publication.
- Be 3,000 to 10,000 words in length and be accompanied by a 600-word précis (in English, even if the paper is written in a different language).

For more information about the 1997 Call for Exemplary Papers, including the criteria by which papers will be judged, you may write to:

Exemplary Papers Program Director
JOHN TEMPLETON FOUNDATION
(http://www.templeton.org)
P.O. Box 8322 • Radnor, PA 19087-8322 USA

Concilium Subscription Information - outside North America

Individual Annual Subscription (five issues): £25.00

Institution Annual Subscription (five issues): £35.00

Airmail subscriptions: add £10.00

Individual issues: £8.95 each

New subscribers please return this form:
for a two-year subscription, double the appropriate rate

(for individuals)   £25.00   (1/2 years)   . . . .

(for institutions)   £35.00   (1/2 years)   . . . .

Airmail postage
outside Europe +£10.00   (1/2 years)   . . . .

                                  Total . . . .

I wish to subscribe for one/two years as an individual/institution
(delete as appropriate)

Name/Institution . . . .

Address . . . .

. . . .

. . . .

I enclose a cheque for . . . . payable to SCM Press Ltd

Please charge my Access/Visa/Mastercard no. . . . .

Signature . . . . .Expiry Date . . . .

Please return this form to:
SCM PRESS LTD   9 - 17 St Albans Place   London   N1 0NX